Fishy Gospel

Richmond Shee

Scripture quotations are from the King James Authorized Version.

Many thanks to Keith Sagayaga for the cover and inside artwork.

ISBN-13: 978-0-578-89184-2

Purple
dreamer
Publishers

With gratitude to the Lord Jesus Christ for the gifts of eternal life and wisdom, and to my beloved wife, Jody.

"Thine, O LORD, is the greatness, and the power, and the glory, and the victory, and the majesty: for all that is in the heaven and in the earth is thine; thine is the kingdom, O LORD, and thou art exalted as head above all."
1Chronicles 29:11

Table of Contents

Preface

History meets the eye on every page of the Bible, which was written by 40 men in various languages and locations over the course of 1,600 years. Most of these authors never met each other, yet they produced 66 books that were harmoniously written, as if by a single author. This is due to the Holy Spirit inspiring these faithful individuals to document God's truth.

In addition to its historical significance, the Bible is also an inspirational book that allows readers to relate to the stories and passages and apply them to their own lives. For instance, consider the story of God commanding Abraham to sacrifice his son Isaac in Genesis 22. How would we react if we were in Isaac's place? Would we have the obedience to follow through with the sacrifice, even if it meant death? What can we learn about trusting God through this story?

Lastly, and most importantly, the Bible is a doctrinal and prophetic book, revealing God's truth and plans for the future. *2Timothy 3:16 All scripture is given by inspiration of God, and is profitable for **doctrine**, for reproof, for correction, for instruction in righteousness. 17 That the man of God may be perfect, throughly furnished unto all good works.* Notice that doctrine leads the way, and if we strive to be mature in our understanding of God's word, we must study doctrine.

The apostle Paul said to Timothy, *"But thou hast fully known my **doctrine**, manner of life, purpose, faith, longsuffering, charity, patience, persecutions, afflictions, which came unto me at Antioch, at Iconium, at Lystra; what persecutions I endured: but out of them* *all the Lord delivered me."* (2Timothy 3:10-11) Notice that Paul was known more for his doctrine than his hobbies, attitude, and other aspects of his life.

Doctrine encompasses God's teachings, including His nature, actions, expectations of us, and future plans, which are also referred to as prophecies. Understanding God's agenda can guide us in living a righteous life and devoting ourselves to studying His word and fulfilling His missions.

"Fishy Gospel" is a serious verse-by-verse commentary on the biblical book of Jonah, encompassing all three aspects of the Bible: historical, inspirational, and prophetic/doctrinal. This book serves as a valuable reference and demonstrates an effective approach to outlining and studying the Bible. It is also recommended as a suitable gift for evangelizing the lost, as the story of Jonah is widely recognized and the message of salvation is prominently featured throughout the book, particularly in Appendix A.

Bible students will uncover the incredible connection between the prophet Jonah and Jesus Christ. They will also gain insight into the future of the nation of Israel in the end times.

Background

If a foreign nation repeatedly invaded your country, raped women, murdered children, destroyed homes and livelihoods, and enslaved people, could you still share the love of God with this enemy?

The Assyrians repeatedly attacked Israel, ultimately bringing about the downfall of the Northern Kingdom. If you were a Jew living in Israel at that time, how would you feel about the Assyrians? Would you embrace them with love or defend yourself with weapons? It was in such a time that God tasked Jonah with a mission of mercy: to warn the Assyrians of impending judgment if they did not repent. Can you imagine being asked to rescue these wicked people from God's wrath and prevent them from perishing in hell?

Was it appropriate for Jonah, a prophet of God, to disobey the divine command due to the hostility between the nations? How did this play out for him? Well, Jonah completed his mission, but not before he became fish food.

The book of Jonah is fifth in the order of the twelve minor prophets: **Hosea**, Joel, **Amos**, Obadiah, Jonah, **Micah**, Nahum, Habakkuk, **Zephaniah**, **Haggai**, **Zechariah**, and Malachi. The first nine prophets prophesied before Israel went into captivity, and the last three after the Jews returned to their land.

The books are referred to as the Minor Prophets, not because they are less authoritative or insignificant, but because of their shorter length of text. However, these books are full of prophecies that are yet to be fulfilled, much like tiny chili peppers that pack a lot of heat. Of the twelve books, six are dated (in bold) as the authors provided a timeframe for their writings, while the remaining six are undated.

The exact date when Jonah, a native of Gathhepher whose name means "Dove," wrote the book is unknown, but it is known that he lived during the time of the divided kingdom (Israel, consisting of ten tribes in the north, and Judah, consisting of two tribes in the south). His primary ministry was to Israel during the reign of King Jeroboam II, who ruled the Northern Kingdom for 41 years starting around 785 B.C. Jonah was a contemporary of the prophets Amos and Hosea. *2Kings 14:23 In the fifteenth year of Amaziah the son of Joash king of Judah Jeroboam the son of Joash king of Israel began to reign in Samaria, and reigned forty and one years. 24 And he did that which was evil in the sight of the LORD: he departed not from all the sins of Jeroboam the son of Nebat, who made Israel to sin. 25 He restored the coast of Israel from the entering of Hamath unto the sea of the plain, according to the word of the LORD God of Israel, which he spake by the hand of his servant Jonah, the son of Amittai, the prophet, which was of Gathhepher.*

During his service to Israel, God gave Jonah an additional mission: to warn the people of Nineveh, the Gentile nation of Assyria and the enemy of Israel.

The book of Jonah is the most popular among the Minor Prophets among Christians due to its simple and straightforward story, which can be easily understood by children. The prophecies in Jonah are also clearer compared to the cryptic messages found in other Minor Prophets. (The book of Nahum is often paired with the book of Jonah.) Although some may consider the book of Jonah as just a moral fable involving a fish, it is a serious book that demonstrates God's love for Gentile nations during the Old Testament era. It contains end-times prophecies concerning Israel that have yet to be fulfilled and also clearly portrays the gospel message of death, burial, and resurrection, pointing readers towards Jesus Christ.

The blood-red gospel runs through the four chapters of the book of Jonah, highlighting the following truth:

- Chapter 1 characterizes **disobedience**, as everyone is born with a sin nature and disobeys God.

- Chapter 2 characterizes **death**, as all sinners are dead in their sin and the wages of sin is death.

- Chapter 3 characterizes **deliverance** or salvation, as all who accept Jesus Christ as Lord and Savior through faith are saved and delivered from God's wrath. Being born again enables individuals to bear fruit for God.

- Chapter 4 characterizes **discipleship** and fruitfulness, as all born-again believers should be discipled and participate in the work of ministry.

The ancient city of Nineveh was located on the eastern bank of the Tigris River in upper Mesopotamia in the land of Shinar, which today encompasses northwestern Iraq, northeastern Syria, and southeastern Turkey. The city was approximately 550 miles from the mouth of the Tigris River and 250 miles north of Babylon. Today, Mosul, Iraq, which is located on the eastern bank of the Tigris, is built on the ruins of Nineveh.

Nineveh was the metropolis of the Assyrian monarchy and was considered a great city in terms of size, as it was *"an exceeding great city of three days' journey"* (Jonah 3:3b). Based on the typical ancient world journey of 20 miles per day, the city's breadth was estimated to be around 60 miles. Nineveh was also great in terms of population, with over 120,000 children under the age of accountability (Jonah 4:11) and an estimated total population between 600,000 and 1 million. The city was also known for its wealth and power, as described in Nahum 2:9, *"Take ye the spoil of silver, take the spoil of gold: for there is none end of the store and glory out of all the pleasant furniture."* However, Nineveh was also known for its evil works, as stated in Jonah 1:2b, *"For their wickedness is come up before me."*

The land of Shinar continues to be a geyser of evil to this day. It was in this plain that the people built the tower of Babel, as described in Genesis 11:1-9. The land of Shinar was also the birthplace of the first human kingdom, ruled by Nimrod, who was the 13th descendant from Adam, following the line of Noah, Ham, and Cush.

Genesis 10:8 describes Nimrod as *"a mighty one in the earth."* He was a mighty hunter, and his skill gained him the description, *"Even as Nimrod the mighty hunter before the LORD."* He gained followers and became their leader, establishing a kingdom that initially consisted of four cities: Babel (Babylon), Erech, Accad, and Calneh (Genesis 10:1-12). Prophetically, Nimrod represents the antichrist who will hunt down God's people, much like the devil who hunts like a roaring lion. *1Peter 5:8 Be sober, be vigilant; because your adversary the devil, as a roaring lion, walketh about, seeking whom he may devour.*

Asshur, who was the descendant of Noah through Shem, was responsible for building the city of Nineveh in the land of Shinar, which became the capital of the Assyrian empire. He also built the cities of Rehoboth, Calah, and Resen.

Essentially, while Nimrod provided the land, his uncle Asshur built the great city of Nineveh. This partnership between Nimrod and Asshur raises the possibility that the antichrist in Revelation could be a mixed black-Jewish person. (Nimrod descended from Ham, the father of dark-skinned peoples, while

Asshur descended from Shem. Abraham, the father of Jews, was also from the line of Shem.)

The land of Nimrod is synonymous with *"the land of Assyria,"* according to Micah 5:6. Interestingly, the Bible also refers to the antichrist as *"the Assyrian"* in Ezekiel 31:1-9.

Today, the original Nineveh lies in ruins, having been destroyed in 612 B.C. by a coalition led by the Babylonians and Medes, which brought down the Assyrian Empire. In 2015 and 2016, the terrorist group ISIS further damaged several ancient sites of Nineveh in Mosul. However, the story is far from over, as the complete fulfillment of the prophecy is yet to come.

The Bible mentions a future role for Nineveh in end times, where the antichrist will arise from it. **Nahum 1:11** *There is one come out of thee* (Nineveh)*, that imagineth evil against the LORD, a wicked counsellor.* It is unclear if this new Nineveh will rise from the ashes of the old or if it is a metaphor for the "great city" mentioned in Revelation 14, 16, 17, and 18. (Many Christians believe that the "great city" is Rome, but this author disagrees. I think the future Nineveh prophesied by the prophets Nahum and Zephaniah [Zephaniah 2:13-15] is the same as "BABYLON THE GREAT" in Revelation and that the city, which will have political authority over the kings of the earth, is still a mystery.)

Jonah wrote this short autobiography, consisting of 48 verses and 1,320 words, that bears his name. He recorded his ministry to the Gentiles of Nineveh and, interestingly, made no mention of Israel. This has caused many Jewish scholars to question the inclusion of the book of Jonah in "The Twelve." However, the reason for its inclusion in the canon of scripture becomes clear when Jesus referenced it in Matthew 12:41, *"The men of Nineveh shall rise in judgment with this generation, and shall condemn it: because they repented at the preaching of Jonas; and, behold, a greater than Jonas is here."* It was meant to admonish the unbelieving Jews. The pagan city of Nineveh repented at the first hearing of God's words, but Israel, a nation of God's chosen people, remained stubborn and uncircumcised in heart and ears, despite numerous reprimands over the generations. (Repentance means to turn around 180 degrees and change from wickedness to righteousness.)

Jonah had multiple personas and served as a sign to both the people of Nineveh and the nation of Israel in Jesus' time. *Luke 11:29 And when the people were gathered thick together, he began to say, This is an evil generation: they seek a sign; and there shall no sign be given it, but the sign of Jonas the prophet. 30 For as Jonas was a sign unto the Ninevites, so shall also the Son of man be to this generation.*

Jonah was the only prophet directly linked to Jesus and acted as a proxy for Him. *Matthew 12:40 For as Jonas was three days and three nights in the whale's belly; so shall the Son of man be three days and three nights in the heart of the earth.* There are many parallels between Jonah and Jesus mentioned throughout this book. This is fascinating as there is not much good that can be said of Jonah, yet we can see Jesus in his life. Likewise, there is not much good that can be said of me, yet I will be like Christ one of these days. God is great!

Jonah was also an anti-type of Christ, as he performed no miracles and showed no compassion. Everything and everyone in the book of Jonah obeyed God, except Jonah himself.

The story of Jonah portrays the current and future state of the nation of Israel:

- Jonah 1 – Disobedient. Presently, Israel is a rebellious nation that rejects their Messiah, Jesus Christ, and refuses to be a light to the Gentiles.

- Jonah 2 – Discipline. Prophetically, Israel will experience great tribulation due to their disobedience and will be deceived and severely persecuted by the antichrist.

- Jonah 3-4 – Deliverance. Prophetically, Israel will realize their error and repent of their sins, accepting Jesus Christ as the Messiah. They will also fulfill God's purpose for their nation, as stated in Isaiah 49:6: *"And he said, It is a light thing that thou shouldest be my servant to raise up the tribes of Jacob, and to restore the preserved of Israel: I will also give thee for a light to the Gentiles, that thou mayest be my salvation unto the end of the earth."* There will be 144,000 Jewish witnesses who will proclaim Jesus as the Messiah during the Great Tribulation period.

Lastly, Jonah is a type of believer who struggles with hatred and needs an attitude adjustment.

1 – "Yes Lord, But…"

Jonah was eager to serve God in Israel, but he refused to go to Nineveh, the capital of the Assyrian empire, to preach. This was due to the long-standing animosity and tension between the two nations, which had resulted in multiple wars.

In the days of King Menahem of Israel, King Pul of Assyria came against Israel. To prevent the invasion, Menahem paid 1,000 talents of silver, which is equivalent to approximately $1.9 million based on a 75-pound weight per talent and $25 per ounce of silver (a substantial sum of money at the time). (Reference: 2Kings 15:19-20)

During the reign of King Pekah of Israel, King Tiglathpileser of Assyria conquered parts of Israel and took the captives to Assyria. (Reference: 2Kings 15:27-29)

King Hoshea of Israel became a servant of King Shalmaneser of Assyria and paid tribute, but when Hoshea became disloyal by forming an alliance with the king of Egypt, King Shalmaneser reinvaded Israel, deported the people, and brought an end to the Northern Kingdom of Israel. (Reference: 2Kings 17, 2Kings 18:9-12)

The above relates to the Northern Kingdom. King Sennacherib of Assyria also invaded the Southern Kingdom of Judah during the reign of King Hezekiah. (Reference: 2Chronicles 32:1-23, Isaiah 36-37, 2Kings 18-19)]

The patriotic prophet of Israel, Jonah, held a strong dislike for the Assyrians and eagerly awaited God's judgment on them. However, when God commanded him to deliver a warning and an opportunity for repentance to the people of Nineveh, Jonah was not at all pleased. He chose to withhold God's mercy from the people by fleeing in the opposite direction, to Tarshish, instead of following God's command. Jonah wanted the Ninevites to face judgment, whereas God wanted them to have a chance at life. ***Jonah 4:1** But it displeased Jonah exceedingly, and he was very angry. ² And he prayed unto the LORD, and said, I pray thee, O LORD, was not this my saying, when I was yet in my country? Therefore I fled before unto Tarshish: for I knew that thou art a gracious God, and merciful, slow to anger, and of great kindness, and repentest thee of the evil. ³ Therefore now, O LORD, take, I beseech thee, my life from me; for it is better for me to die than to live.*

Was Jonah's attitude influenced by prejudice? Did he commit an act of hate by denying the people of Nineveh access to God's warning? How many people do you know who would readily share the gospel with those who have caused them harm? You may not have a mortal enemy like Jonah, but what about a coworker who belittles your faith and constantly undermines you?

All of us have a little bit of Jonah in us. We may be eager to serve God, especially after attending a church retreat or seminar, but when it comes to sharing the gospel with those who have wronged us, we struggle. Like Jonah, we prefer to serve God within our comfort zones and hope that God will not challenge us to step outside of our self-imposed boundaries.

The book of Jonah, Chapter 1, highlights the truth stated in Romans 6:23, which says that the wages of sin is death. Disobedience is sin and leads to death. The following outlines the events in Jonah 1:

- Directive given – Jonah 1:1-2
- Disobedience demonstrated – Jonah 1:3
- Disastrous consequences – Jonah 1:4-17

Jonah 1:1 Now the word of the LORD came unto Jonah the son of Amittai, saying,

Like the Gospel of John, the book of Jonah begins with a word from the Almighty Jehovah God. The phrase *"the word of the LORD came unto"* appears 63 times in the Bible, all in the Old Testament, with a concentration in the books of Jeremiah (12 times) and Ezekiel (37 times). This phrase does not appear in the New Testament because, according to the Gospel of John, the Word had manifested Himself in the person of Jesus Christ.

Jonah briefly introduces himself as the *"the son of Amittai,"* with the name Amittai meaning "my truth." In this sense, the word of the Lord came to the son of truth. ***John 17:17*** *Sanctify them through thy truth: thy word is truth.* Can you see the parallel to yourself? If you have been born again through the word of God, you are a son of truth and God speaks to you directly. ***1Peter 1:23*** *Being born again, not of corruptible seed, but of incorruptible, by the word of God, which liveth and abideth for ever.*

God has something to say to you through the Bible. His written words are authoritative and should be received into the good soil of your heart, obeyed, and lived out through faith. What is your attitude towards God's word? Read Psalm 119:9-16, 97-106.

The presence of the Godhead is evident in Jonah 1:1, with the LORD representing God the Father, the name Amittai ("my truth") representing God the Son, and the name Jonah ("dove") representing God the Holy Spirit.

Jonah 1:2 Arise, go to Nineveh, that great city, and cry against it; for their wickedness is come up before me.

Really God? You want me to prolong the life of an enemy nation that is in the process of exterminating my country? You must be joking, right? Don't you remember what these uncircumcised

Gentiles did to Israel? (This verse shows that God cares for the Gentiles and doesn't want them to die in sin.)

Jonah, the son of truth (Amittai), was commanded to preach to the people of Nineveh. Can we relate to this? The son of truth needs to arise, go, and spread the gospel to the lost. *Mark 16:15 And he said unto them, Go ye into all the world, and preach the gospel to every creature.*

The first order of business is to arise:

- Arise from self-righteousness and put off the old man. Indeed, self-righteousness is the main thing that prevents us from reaching out to sinners. The Pharisees went through the motions of religion and judged themselves better than others. *Luke 18:9 And he spake this parable unto certain which trusted in themselves that they were righteous, and despised others: ¹⁰ Two men went up into the temple to pray; the one a Pharisee, and the other a publican. ¹¹ The Pharisee stood and prayed thus with himself, God, I thank thee, that I am not as other men are, extortioners, unjust, adulterers, or even as this publican. ¹² I fast twice in the week, I give tithes of all that I possess. ¹³ And the publican, standing afar off, would not lift up so much as his eyes unto heaven, but smote upon his breast, saying, God be merciful to me a sinner. ¹⁴ I tell you, this man went down to his house justified rather than the other: for every one that exalteth himself shall be abased; and he that humbleth himself shall be exalted.*

- Arise to walk in the Spirit, in newness of life, and not in the hateful flesh. Put on the new person, which is renewed in knowledge after the image of God. *Colossians 3:12 Put on therefore, as the elect of God, holy and beloved, bowels of mercies, kindness, humbleness of mind, meekness, longsuffering;* [13] *Forbearing one another, and forgiving one another, if any man have a quarrel against any: even as Christ forgave you, so also do ye.*

- Arise to love sinners as God loves them. **Colossians 3:14** *And above all these things put on charity, which is the bond of perfectness.* **John 3:16** *For God so loved the world, that he gave his only begotten Son, that whosoever believeth in him should not perish, but have everlasting life.*

- Arise for the work of ministry. The Lord said to the Apostle Paul, *"Arise, and go into the city* (Damascus).*"* He said to Ananias, *"Arise, and go into the street which is called Straight."* (Acts 9:6, 11) The Lord also commanded Philip the evangelist, *"Arise, and go toward the south unto the way that goeth down from Jerusalem unto Gaza, which is desert."* (Acts 8:26) In the Old Testament, He commanded the prophet Jeremiah, *"Arise, and go down to the potter's house."* (Jeremiah 18:2) All these men obeyed Him. How do we respond to Mark 16:15?

Next, we must go. The command is for the church to reach out to the world, not the other way around. Some churches teach that Christians should live a pure life so that sinners will come to them, but the Bible is clear—we must go. But where to? How about Nineveh? Although the ancient city no longer exists, it represents a world full of sinners. We must go to our neighbors, towns, cities, and distant places. **Acts 1:8** *But ye shall receive power, after that the Holy Ghost is come upon you: and ye shall be witnesses unto me both in Jerusalem, and in all Judaea, and in Samaria, and unto the uttermost part of the earth.* Listen to the hymns, "Go ye into all the world" by James McGranahan, and "A passion for souls" by Herbert Tovey and Foss Fellers.

Many souls are in danger of perishing. ***Matthew 7:13** Enter ye in at the strait gate: for wide is the gate, and broad is the way, that leadeth to destruction, and many there be which go in thereat: ^{14} Because strait is the gate, and narrow is the way, which leadeth unto life, and few there be that find it.* But God, who is *"not willing that any should perish, but that all should come to repentance,"* has committed to us the ministry of reconciliation. ***2Corinthians 5:18** And all things are of God, who hath reconciled us to himself by Jesus Christ, and hath given to us the ministry of reconciliation; ^{19} To wit, that God was in Christ, reconciling the world unto himself, not imputing their trespasses unto them; and hath committed unto us the word of reconciliation. ^{20} Now then we are ambassadors for Christ, as though God did beseech you by us: we pray you in Christ's stead, be ye reconciled to God. ^{21} For he hath made him to be sin for us, who knew no sin; that we might be made the righteousness of God in him.*

Observe the disparity between God's view and Jonah's view of the Assyrians in Nineveh. From Jonah's perspective, they were deadly enemies who deserved God's judgment. But according to Jonah 4:11, God saw the Assyrians as people in need of a Savior. From God's viewpoint, both the Assyrians and Israelites had sinned. Out of the 19 kings of the northern tribes of Israel, how many were good? None. They were all wicked kings who did evil in the sight of the Lord and provoked His anger. This span lasted from Jeroboam the son of Nebat to the last king Hoshea, a total of 254 years (the division of the kingdom began in 975 B.C. and the Assyrian captivity was in 721 B.C.).

God was patient with Israel. He chastised Israel by delivering them into the hands of spoilers and selling them into the hands of their enemies, but Israel was stiff-necked and never repented of their sins. ***1Kings 14:16** And he shall give Israel up because of the sins of Jeroboam, who did sin, and who made Israel to sin.*

Jonah's nearsightedness towards his nation's circumstances obscured his vision of God's kingdom. We too can lose sight of God's kingdom if we focus too much on our own circumstances.

Before we can reach out to sinners, we must acknowledge that we are sinners as well, in accordance with Romans 3:23, *"For all have sinned, and come short of the glory of God."* We may never have committed a heinous sin, but any sin is still a sin. The punishment for sin is the same for everyone—death, according to Romans 6:23. This puts us on the same level as the worst criminal. Only then can we see things from God's perspective and be able to minister to all people, even our enemies. We may hate our enemies, but God says, *"Love your enemies, bless them that curse you, do good to them that hate you, and pray for them which despitefully use you, and persecute you."* (Matthew 5:44) We may wish death on our enemies, but God wishes life on both. We may withhold mercy from our enemies, but God says, *"If thine enemy be hungry, give him bread to eat; and if he be thirsty, give him water to drink."* (Proverbs 25:21)

Winning souls requires a selfless and sacrificial mindset. It is important to put aside personal opinions and biases, and to focus on the truth of God's message. As it is written, *"Let God be true, but every man a liar."*

In Christianity, dying to one's own self is a fundamental aspect of the faith. **Luke 9:20** *He said unto them, But whom say ye that I am? Peter answering said, The Christ of God.* [21] *And he straitly charged them, and commanded them to tell no man that thing;* [22] *Saying, The Son of man must suffer many things, and be rejected of the elders and chief priests and scribes, and be slain, and be raised the third day.* [23] *And he said to them all, If any man will come after me, let him deny himself, and take up his cross daily, and follow me.* **John 12:24** *Verily, verily, I say unto you, Except a corn of wheat fall into the ground and die, it abideth alone: but if it die, it bringeth forth much fruit.*

The world is a better place when Jesus Christ is at the center of each person's heart. Our mission is to share the gospel with everyone, even those who may be considered notorious. In 2008/2009, Christians in Odisha, India faced severe persecution from Hindus. Many were murdered, others were beaten and had their homes burned down, resulting in the loss of their livelihood. I had the opportunity to preach the gospel in Odisha on three separate occasions, and during my first visit, I met a man who had been imprisoned, beaten, and subjected to torture because of his faith in Christ. His jailer even made him drink his own urine as a form of punishment. Despite these difficult circumstances, this man remained steadfast in his faith and shared the gospel with his jailer, who eventually became a believer and a brother in Christ. This man understood that his enemies were not physical beings, but rather spiritual forces, and that he was in jail for the purpose of spreading the gospel to the jailer, whose sins were known to God—*"for their wickedness is come up before me."* **Ephesians 6:12** *For we wrestle not against flesh and blood, but against principalities, against powers, against the rulers of the darkness of this world, against spiritual wickedness in high places.*

While in Philippi, the Apostle Paul was imprisoned for preaching the gospel. However, this difficult experience turned out to be for the salvation of the Philippian jailer, as described in Acts 16:25-32.

God sent Jonah to warn the Ninevites because their sins had piled up to high heaven, as it is written *"for their wickedness is come up before me."* The world is full of sinners, from those in high positions to those considered to be the lowest of society. Some people's sins are blatantly obvious, while some are hidden. **1Timothy 5:24** *Some men's sins are open beforehand, going before to judgment; and some men they follow after.* Nasty people need Christ the most. **Mark 2:17** *When Jesus heard it, he saith unto them, They that are whole have no need of the physician, but they that are sick: I came not to call the righteous, but sinners to repentance.* God is searching for faithful servants to share the gospel with those who are stubborn, reject Christ, oppose the truth, and are considered "nasty." Do we expect God to send us only to those who are receptive and welcoming? No, it is the sinners who are our mission field.

Are you able to share the gospel of salvation and lead sinners to Christ? If you feel intimidated or afraid to do so, remember that Jesus Himself engaged with people who ultimately sought to kill him. John 10:32 provides guidance on how to avoid harm. **John 10:31** *Then the Jews took up stones again to stone him. ³² Jesus answered them, Many good works have I shewed you from my Father; for which of those works do ye stone me? ³³ The Jews answered him, saying, For a good work we stone thee not; but for blasphemy; and because that thou, being a man, makest thyself God.*

The Bible states, "*We are his workmanship, created in Christ Jesus unto good works, which God hath before ordained that we should walk in them*" (Ephesians 2:10). By prefacing our message with mercy (good works), we can safely share the gospel (truth) with sinners. In the Bible, mercy and truth are intertwined and cannot be separated. Mercy without truth is simply social work, while truth without mercy can be cruel. Notice how Luke 24:19 describes Jesus, "*And he said unto them, What things? And they said unto him, Concerning Jesus of Nazareth, which was a prophet mighty in <u>deed and word</u> before God and all the people.*"

May God equip you for His service and prosper you with fruit that remains. **Romans 10:15** *And how shall they preach, except they be sent? as it is written, How beautiful are the feet of them that preach the gospel of peace, and bring glad tidings of good things!*

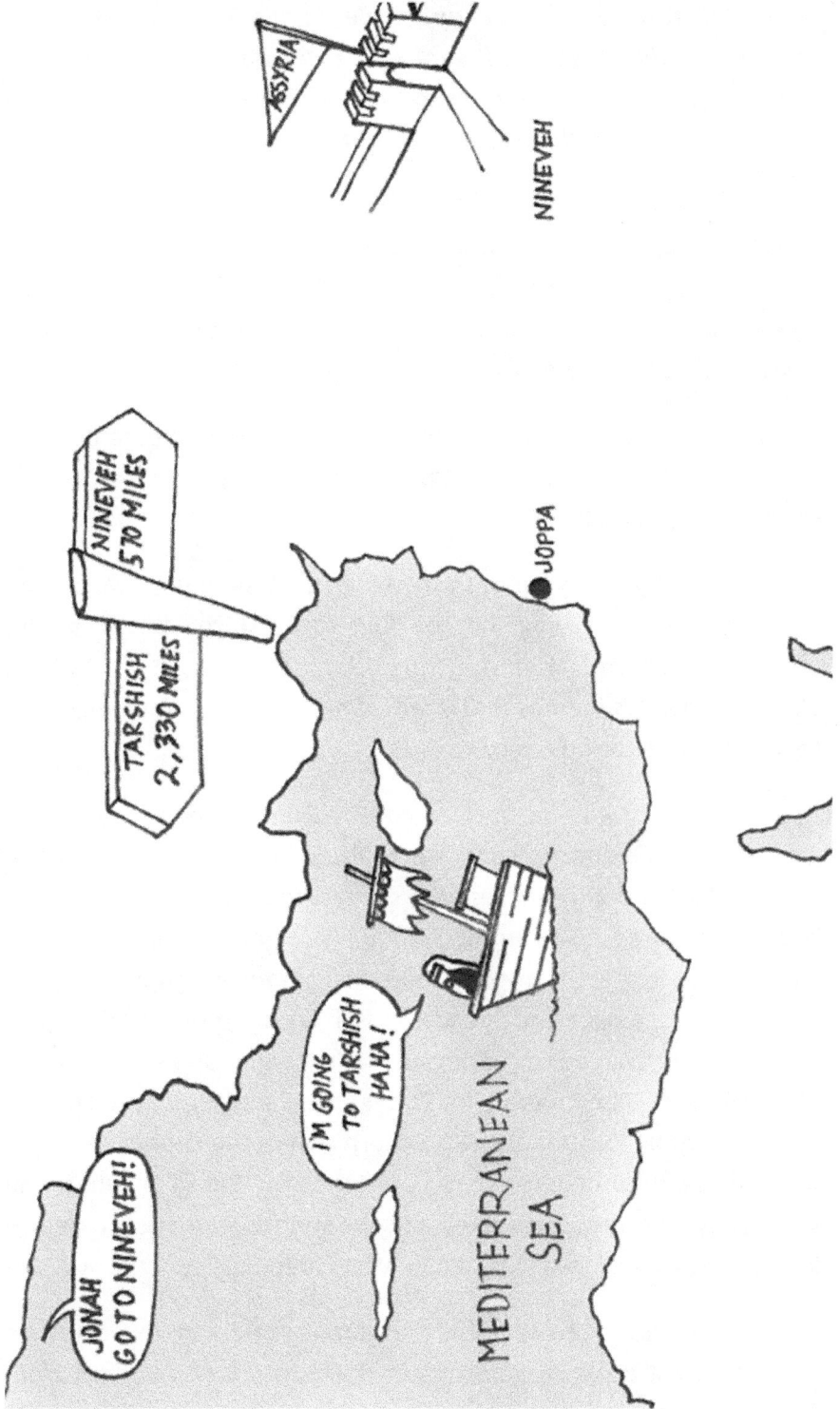

Jonah 1:3 But Jonah rose up to flee unto Tarshish from the presence of the LORD, and went down to Joppa; and he found a ship going to Tarshish: so he paid the fare thereof, and went down into it, to go with them unto Tarshish from the presence of the LORD.

The authoritative commandment of Jehovah God was met with resistance in the form of "But." Jonah's response was essentially, "Not on my watch!" How many of us would say, "Jesus loves you," to those we dislike?

It is not wise to respond to God's commandments with "But." We may know what the Bible says, but... A pastor I know likes to say, "Your buts stink."

Jonah got two out of three things right: he didn't waste time in getting up and going, but he fled to Tarshish—the complete opposite direction of Nineveh. This is like the prodigal son in Luke 15, who *"took his journey into a far country,"* to be as far away from his loving father as possible.

Tarshish was an ancient city believed to be located near modern-day Gibraltar in southern Spain. However, the accounts in 1Kings 10:22 and 2Chronicles 9:21 suggest that Tarshish might have been in Africa or India. During Solomon's reign, his ships made the long journey to Tarshish every three years and returned with gold, silver, ivory, apes, and peacocks. Sixty or more years after Solomon's reign, during Jehoshaphat's reign, ships bound for Tarshish were constructed in Eziongeber (modern-day Eilat), an ancient seaport located at the northern end of the Gulf of Aqaba of the Red Sea, according to 2Chronicles 20:35-36. Based on where the ships were built, their cargoes, and the maritime voyage, it seems logical that Tarshish was located in Africa or India.

Jonah sailed to Tarshish from Joppa, a port town located on the southwest coast of Palestine in the territory of Dan, not from Eziongeber. Before the opening of the Suez Canal, ships from

Eziongeber would have had to sail around the African continent to reach the coast of Israel in the Mediterranean Sea. If Tarshish was in southern Spain, it wouldn't make sense for the ships to be constructed in Eziongeber. Would the ancient people have transported the ships over land, a distance of about 170 miles as the crow flies, from Eziongeber to Joppa? Was it because the necessary skill and labor were only available in Eziongeber? However, the main raw material, timber, was plentiful in Lebanon. In the past, timbers were floated by sea from Lebanon to Joppa, according to 2Chronicles 2:16 and Ezra 3:7. Wouldn't it have been easier to bring the skill and labor to the timber, rather than vice versa?

Tarshish was also the name of Noah's great-grandson (Noah -> Japheth -> Javan -> Tarshish) from Japheth's line, who was the father of the Europeans. If the city was founded by and named after him, then Tarshish might have been a city in a distant part of the Mediterranean Sea.

Assuming Tarshish was near Gibraltar, the distance from Joppa to Nineveh was about 570 miles, and from Joppa to Tarshish was about 2,330 miles as the crow flies. Our disobedience takes us far away in the opposite direction of God's will. We should be moving in the opposite direction of the world. Unfortunately, many Christians are trying to blend in with the world. Is a lighthouse relevant if it becomes as dark as the night? *2Corinthians 4:6 For God, who commanded the light to shine out of darkness, hath shined in our hearts, to give the light of the knowledge of the glory of God in the face of Jesus Christ. Philippians 2:15 That ye may be blameless and harmless, the sons of God, without rebuke, in the midst of a crooked and perverse nation, among whom ye shine as lights in the world.*

Do we want to be like many of the world's lighthouses that have stopped functioning and now serve only as tourist attractions? "Come see us, we're useless."

If God is speaking to your heart, don't stand still or run away. Like Jonah, you may have elaborate plans to avoid serving God, but the outcome will be disastrous. Are you willing to pay the price of going in the wrong direction?

Jonah *"went down"* to Joppa to catch the fastest mode of transportation available at the time. The name Joppa means "beautiful." Today, the town is known as Jaffa, and the modern city of Tel Aviv to its north has annexed it and was renamed Tel Aviv-Yafo. Joppa was a bustling port of Jerusalem during Solomon's reign. It was also where the Apostle Peter received a message from the Lord that Gentiles could be saved. (Read the story of Cornelius in Acts 10.)

It was a beautiful day, with a blue sky and white puffy clouds, the perfect weather for sailing. There was no storm forecast. Life was good! Jonah bought a ticket and *"went down"* into a ship. (In Jonah 1:5, he had *"gone down into the sides of the ship"* to sleep. Later, in Jonah 2:6, he died—*"went down to the bottoms of the mountains."*) That's the three "downs" of a sinner. The first "down" is disobedience and departure from God. The second "down" is the captivity of sin. The third "down" is physical death for not repenting.

Do we think we can sail away from the Lord's presence and avoid fulfilling our duties towards Him? Evangelism is not just for gifted evangelists, it is what all Christians are called to do. Evangelism should be our passion and the focus of our prayers. The lesson here is that if God asks us to do something and we disobey, we will go down in misery. Like Jonah, our disobedience may even cost us our lives.

In our disobedience, we will always be able to find a means readily available to take us away from serving God. In Jonah's case, he found a ship bound for his rebellious destination. If we ever need an excuse for not serving God, we will easily find one. Here's a test question: why don't we evangelize and disciple more people? See the reasons (excuses) that pop up in our minds? When was the last time we shared the gospel with someone? Have we spent four to five hours this week (or this month) doing work for the kingdom, or are we too busy pursuing worldly things and not affecting anyone's life for Christ? Our "stinky buts" are preventing us from being useful to God.

Note that Jonah paid the fare. If we obey God, He will pave the way and pay the fare, but if we disobey Him, we will pay for our rebellion.

We will also find companions who will join us on our journey to Tarshish, which represents our chosen escape destination. We will not be alone. These people will agree with us on why we should live for ourselves instead of serving God.

Jonah 1:3 is the tipping verse. What follows was hell for Jonah. Just one act of disobedience and the rest was a series of disastrous consequences. Jesus Christ gave His life for our sins. If we are born again in Him but choose to live for ourselves and ignore His kingdom, then *"prepare to meet thy God."* (Amos 4:12b) Let us be forever grateful for Jesus' great sacrifice and fulfill our duty to God. *John 14:12 Verily, verily, I say unto you, He that believeth on me, the works that I do shall he do also; and greater works than these shall he do; because I go unto my Father.*

2 – The "But" Showdown in the Mediterranean Sea

Jonah's "but" of disobedience made him a fugitive prophet. As he was running away from God towards Tarshish in a ship, God was in hot pursuit. God also had a "but," and the showdown resulted in Jonah's death.

This chapter shows that God never gives up on His servants, even when they disobey and bring dishonor to Him. God will arrange events to bring them to repentance.

The following is an outline of Jonah 1:4-17:

- God pursues Jonah – Jonah 1:4-6
- God exposes Jonah – Jonah 1:7-10
- God arrests Jonah – Jonah 1:11-17

Jonah 1:4 But the LORD sent out a great wind into the sea, and there was a mighty tempest in the sea, so that the ship was like to be broken.

When we throw our "but" of disobedience at God, He too can throw one back at us, except that His is much bigger.

God had many things at His disposal, but He chose the wind. Not just any wind, but a great wind. The Hebrew word for wind here is "רוח," which is also translated as "Spirit." The first mention of this word is in Genesis 1:2b, *"And the Spirit (רוח) of God moved upon the face of the waters."* When the Spirit of God moves, He renovates, enlightens, intercedes, and draws people to God. Indeed, Jonah needed some attitude adjustments. The Spirit of God caused a mighty tempest in the sea, and the waves beat so hard against the ship that it was in danger of breaking apart. Unrepentant sinners, especially those who belong to God, can expect a Pursuer with His disquieting storms and tempests (physical and spiritual) in their lives.

However, it started as a beautiful day, and everything was calm until Jonah sailed away. We might say that God showed a buffer of grace between the initial rebellion and sailing away. He gives us time and space to repent and turn away from sin and evil. If we don't, the Holy Spirit will come after us and rock our boat. **Hebrews 10:31** *It is a fearful thing to fall into the hands of the living God.*

Do you know who can calm the raging tempest in your soul? **Luke 8:22** *Now it came to pass on a certain day, that he went into a ship with his disciples: and he said unto them, Let us go over unto the other side of the lake. And they launched forth.* [23] *But as they sailed he fell asleep: and there came down a storm of wind on the lake; and they were filled with water, and were in jeopardy.* [24] *And they came to him, and awoke him, saying, Master, master, we perish. Then he arose, and rebuked the wind and the raging of the water: and they ceased, and there was a calm.* [25] *And he said unto them, Where is your faith? And they being afraid wondered, saying one to another, What manner of man is this! for he commandeth even the winds and water, and they obey him.*

If you have strayed away, return to the Lord. Perhaps your experience with God is based on religion and not on a personal relationship with His Son, Jesus Christ. If that's the case, see "How to Accept Jesus Christ as Lord and Savior" in Appendix A.

Jonah 1:5 Then the mariners were afraid, and cried every man unto his god, and cast forth the wares that were in the ship into the sea, to lighten it of them. But Jonah was gone down into the sides of the ship; and he lay, and was fast asleep.

How would you like to be in the same boat as the sinner that God is after and become collateral damage? The experienced mariners saw the massive waves and knew they were in trouble. In terror, they called out to their little "g" gods. And when their gods did not answer their prayers (how could they, according to Psalm 115:4-8), they dumped their cargo into the sea in desperation to lighten the ship and preserve their lives. (Notice the progression from eyes to hearts to mouths to hands.)

Beware of the god you pray to when you're in trouble. If you pray to the wrong one, you will have much to lose and make no progress.

Unrepentant sinners are dangerous to themselves, their loved ones, and the people around them. Besides hurting themselves physically, mentally, and financially, they put great strain on relationships. Lives and livelihoods are jeopardized by one sinner's sins, which often start with family members and spread to society.

All hands were on deck, except for Jonah who was fast asleep in the inner part of the ship, completely unconcerned with the danger he posed to others. Jonah knew that God was after him—*"for I know that for my sake this great tempest is upon you."* He didn't care if he died or took others down with him. This is the attitude of many unrepentant sinners who are aware that they are going down and don't mind if others go down with them.

How could Jonah be so sound asleep in such a dire situation? Sin puts us into a carnal slumber and makes us indifferent to our surroundings. Sin also leads to a false sense of security that we are beyond God's reach, so we continue on. When we reach this state, intervention is necessary, as we see in the following verses.

(In a similar manner, Jesus was also asleep in a boat while crossing the Lake Gennesaret with His disciples. They also encountered a life-threatening storm before Jesus rebuked the wind and calmed the sea. Read about the account in Matthew 8:23-27, Mark 4:35-41, Luke 8:22-25.)

Jonah 1:6 So the shipmaster came to him, and said unto him, What meanest thou, O sleeper? arise, call upon thy God, if so be that God will think upon us, that we perish not.

Anticipating a shipwreck, the captain of the ship searched for passengers and found Jonah sleeping. The Hebrew word for "sleeper" is "רדם," is also translated as "dead sleep" in Psalm 76:6. The captain was shocked to find Jonah so unaware of the dangerous situation and woke him up, asking, "What do you mean you're asleep?" The captain's next sentence was *"Arise, call upon thy God."* This was brilliant advice from a pagan, whose statement acknowledged that his patron god was inferior to the Almighty God and that he did not have a personal relationship with Him. Despite this, the captain's motives were good; he did not want anyone to perish, saying, *"if so be that God will think upon us, that we perish not."* It's amazing that a pagan desired life more than the servant of God, who had abandoned his cause and was indifferent to life.

Pause and reflect on this. In order to not perish, one must call upon God. What verses come to mind? ***2Peter 3:9*** *The Lord is not slack concerning his promise, as some men count slackness; but is longsuffering to us-ward, not willing that any should perish, but that all should come to repentance.* ***John 3:16*** *For God so loved the world, that he gave his only begotten Son, that whosoever believeth in him should not perish, but have everlasting life.*

The advice to *"Arise, call upon thy God"* is also profound. It's better to avoid a shipwreck, but if we ever find ourselves in one, we must call upon God.

A similar call to awaken is made to backsliding Christians who are not involved in ministry. **Ephesians 5:14** *Wherefore he saith, Awake thou that sleepest, and arise from the dead, and Christ shall give thee light. ¹⁵ See then that ye walk circumspectly, not as fools, but as wise, ¹⁶ Redeeming the time, because the days are evil. ¹⁷ Wherefore be ye not unwise, but understanding what the will of the Lord is.*

It's just as surprising to find a blood-washed Christian who is disengaged from ministry and unwilling to support the cause of Christ, as it was for the shipmaster to find Jonah fast asleep. To these individuals, I say, *"What meanest thou, O sleeper?"* Many people will perish if we don't rise from our flowery beds of ease.

Jonah 1:7 And they said every one to his fellow, Come, and let us cast lots, that we may know for whose cause this evil is upon us. So they cast lots, and the lot fell upon Jonah.

The scene changes from a call to prayer to a call for a witch hunt. The situation was so dire that the mariners referred to it as *"evil."* They believed that one of their shipmates might have committed a terrible sin to attract such evil, so they gathered everyone to cast lots to uncover the culprit.

The casting of lots was a Jewish practice of seeking God's will, first used by Aaron, the high priest, as described in Leviticus 16:8. The heathen, who were unfamiliar with the true God, adopted and used the practice, not realizing they were appealing to the Almighty. As prophesied in Psalm 22:18, the heathen cast lots for the vesture of the Son of God, and this is exactly what the soldiers did when they cast lots for Jesus' vesture after having crucified Him (John 19:24).

After Pentecost, there is no further mention of casting lots. As New Testament Christians, we do not rely on the casting of lots to know God's will. We have His will in the Bible.

Are you surprised that the lot fell on Jonah? God has a way of exposing sinners. The Bible says, *"Be sure your sin will find you out."* For example, the prophet Nathan said to David, *"Thou art the man,"* revealing his guilt for adultery and murder. God will expose sinners with or without the lot system. Should we continue to hide our sins? **Proverbs 28:13** *He that covereth his sins shall not prosper: but whoso confesseth and forsaketh them shall have mercy.*

Jonah 1:8 Then said they unto him, Tell us, we pray thee, for whose cause this evil is upon us; What is thine occupation? and whence comest thou? what is thy country? and of what people art thou? ⁹ And he said unto them, I am an Hebrew; and I fear the LORD, the God of heaven, which hath made the sea and the dry land. ¹⁰ Then were the men exceedingly afraid, and said unto him, Why hast thou done this? For the men knew that he fled from the presence of the LORD, because he had told them.

By this point, most people would have confronted Jonah and demanded to know what he had done to cause such evil. But the mariners were kind to him, *"Tell us, we pray thee."* They interrogated him with four consecutive questions: What is your occupation? Where are you from? What is your country? And what is your nationality? The mariners were interested in Jonah's abilities, rather than the crime he was guilty of, perhaps because he was indifferent, and they thought that if he had the power to cause such a powerful storm, he also had the power to calm it.

Jonah's confession was essentially this: "I am a Hebrew and I am afraid, as I am being pursued by Jehovah, the Creator of the sea and dry land, whom the sea obeys."

The mariners were already afraid of their situation (Jonah 1:5), but now they were even more afraid for their lives, having become associated with the fugitive who was being pursued by the angry God of heaven.

They said to Jonah, *"Why hast thou done this?"* not because they expected an answer, but to rebuke him. It was foolish of Jonah to run away from God, putting them in such distress and danger. Imagine, even the heathen knew better than to neglect their duty to God. How many Christians are serving God today, and how many are inactive? To fellow Christians who are avoiding serving God, *"Why hast thou done this?"*

Jonah 1:11 Then said they unto him, What shall we do unto thee, that the sea may be calm unto us? for the sea wrought, and was tempestuous. ¹² And he said unto them, Take me up, and cast me forth into the sea; so shall the sea be calm unto you: for I know that for my sake this great tempest is upon you. ¹³ Nevertheless the men rowed hard to bring it to the land; but they could not: for the sea wrought, and was tempestuous against them.

With the root cause of the storm now understood, the mariners' final question to Jonah was, *"What shall we do unto thee, that the sea may be calm unto us?"* This was because Jonah was not going to take any action to improve the situation, and the sea continued to become more violent.

The solution was obvious: Jonah must die. However, there was a problem: Jonah was not going to kill himself by jumping off the ship. He wanted the mariners to throw him overboard, but the mariners did not want to commit murder. So they tried hard to bring the ship to land, but their efforts were in vain as they were no match for the Almighty God.

Tired of a tumultuous life? Did you know that there is a Jonah in each one of us? This disobedient character draws us away from serving God and gets us into trouble with Him—*"for I know that for my sake this great tempest is upon you."* Interestingly, Jonah wants to die (Jonah 4:3, 8), but he will not take his own life. We must throw the Jonah within us overboard and return to serving God to restore peace.

Jonah 1:14 Wherefore they cried unto the LORD, and said, We beseech thee, O LORD, we beseech thee, let us not perish for this man's life, and lay not upon us innocent blood: for thou, O LORD, hast done as it pleased thee.

The exhausted mariners did everything they could to save their lives, but found themselves in a difficult situation. They realized that God would not be appeased until He captured His subject, and the only way they could save themselves was to throw Jonah overboard, as he had instructed in verse 12. No captain would want that on his record.

If Jonah did not die, they would all die, but if Jonah were to die, they would all live. Do you see the parallel with Jesus Christ? We are doomed if Jesus did not die on the cross to pay the penalty for our sins. We live because He died for our sins and rose again.

Even though Jonah was the cause of their problems and losses, his actions were not deserving of death. These mariners did not want to shed "innocent blood." (God hates those who shed innocent blood. ***Exodus 23:7** Keep thee far from a false matter; and the innocent and righteous slay thou not: for I will not justify the wicked.* ***Proverbs 6:16** These six things doth the LORD hate: yea, seven are an abomination unto him:* [17] *A proud look, a lying tongue,* *and hands that shed innocent blood.*) Therefore, the mariners begged God for their lives and for mercy—*"let us not perish for this man's life, and lay not upon us innocent blood."* The mariners also acknowledged that God was sovereign, as it was clear to them that things happened according to His will and not theirs. *Psalm 115:3 But our God is in the heavens: he hath done whatsoever he hath pleased.*

The phrase *"innocent blood"* is unmistakably a reference to Jesus Christ. *Matthew 27:1 When the morning was come, all the chief priests and elders of the people took counsel against Jesus to put him to death: ² And when they had bound him, they led him away, and delivered him to Pontius Pilate the governor. ³ Then Judas, which had betrayed him, when he saw that he was condemned, repented himself, and brought again the thirty pieces of silver to the chief priests and elders, ⁴ Saying, I have sinned in that I have betrayed the innocent blood. And they said, What is that to us? see thou to that. Psalm 94:21 They gather themselves together against the soul of the righteous, and condemn the innocent blood.* We have all sinned, but the innocent blood of the righteous Jesus Christ is available to cleanse us of our sins.

Jonah 1:15 So they took up Jonah, and cast him forth into the sea: and the sea ceased from her raging. ¹⁶ Then the men feared the LORD exceedingly, and offered a sacrifice unto the LORD, and made vows.

If someone held you over the side of a ship in a stormy sea, wouldn't that be the moment to say, "Wait, wait, I give up?" Not Jonah. He remained unrepentant to the end, fully embracing his disobedience. So, the mariners threw him overboard, and the sea became calm. The sudden change from a mighty tempest to great calm must have been freaky, and they probably all fell to their knees. *Psalm 107:23 They that go down to the sea in ships, that do business in great waters; ²⁴ These see the works of the LORD, and his wonders in the deep. ²⁵ For he commandeth, and raiseth the stormy wind, which lifteth up the waves thereof. ²⁶ They mount up to the heaven, they go down again to the depths: their soul is melted because of trouble. ²⁷ They reel to and fro, and stagger like a drunken man, and are at their wits' end. ²⁸ Then they cry unto the LORD in their trouble, and he bringeth them out of their distresses. ²⁹ He maketh the storm a calm, so that the waves thereof are still. ³⁰ Then are they glad because they be quiet; so he bringeth them unto their desired haven. ³¹ Oh that men would praise the LORD for his goodness, and for his wonderful works to the children of men!*

There are three lessons to be learned from this story:

1. We must be led by the Spirit of God, not by the Jonah within us, as he will continue to disobey God to the end.

2. Peace can only be achieved through God's way. The mariners dumped cargo into the sea, but nothing happened. The sea became peaceful when they followed Jonah's instructions in verse 12.

3. Sinners will meet their demise in their sinful path.

The mariners' fear of God changed. In Jonah 1:5 and 10, they were afraid of their situation and for their lives. In verse 15, they became exceedingly afraid of the Lord. They went from "Oh my God, what's happening" to "Oh my God, we are going to die" to "Oh God Almighty."

Their fear of God led them to offer a sacrifice and make vows. While this may not have been a wise decision, I hope they fulfilled their vows. **Ecclesiastes 5:5** *Better is it that thou shouldest not vow, than that thou shouldest vow and not pay. ⁶ Suffer not thy mouth to cause thy flesh to sin; neither say thou before the angel, that it was an error: wherefore should God be angry at thy voice, and destroy the work of thine hands?*

The wrath of God was appeased when Jonah was sacrificed. Just as Jonah was lifted up before he died, Jesus Christ was also lifted up and suspended in midair on the cross. You too, can appease God by accepting Jesus Christ's finished work on the cross.

As Jonah was killed by Gentiles, Jesus Christ was crucified by the Romans.

3 – From Sushi to Salvation

God had a special sushi reception for Jonah. The fresh and live sushi ate Jonah instead. He was inside the fish's belly for three days and three nights, but God miraculously preserved his body from the gastric acid. The poor fish experienced serious indigestion for about 72 hours. By the grace of God, Jonah repented of his sin.

Jonah chapter 2 paints a beautiful picture of death, burial, and resurrection, which is an incredible parallel to Jesus Christ. The resurrection from death is the wonder of wonders, and any attempt to remove the book of Jonah from the canon of scripture is an attack on the most wonderful thing that can ever happen to a condemned sinner.

Jonah chapter 2 offers hope to backsliders and sinners who are ready to repent. Psalms 86:5 says, *"For thou, Lord, art good, and ready to forgive; and plenteous in mercy unto all them that call upon thee."* His grace abounds and is far greater than our sins.

The chapter can be outlined as such:

- A hope for God's hearing – Jonah 2:1-3
- A hope for God sighting – Jonah 2:4-5
- A hope for incorruptible life – Jonah 2:6-7
- A hope to return to service – Jonah 2:8-10

Jonah 1:17 Now the LORD had prepared a great fish to swallow up Jonah. And Jonah was in the belly of the fish three days and three nights.

The fugitive prophet was finally arrested, but God was always one step ahead. He had already thought about and prepared the next steps for Jonah.

God also has our next steps planned out depending on our relationship with Him. *Proverbs 16:9 A man's heart deviseth his way: but the LORD directeth his steps. Proverbs 20:24 Man's goings are of the LORD; how can a man then understand his own way? Psalm 37:23 The steps of a good man are ordered by the LORD: and he delighteth in his way.*

If we fall away from Him, we should be cautious of the *"great fish,"* which could be anything that consumes us in our sins. Just like Jonah, we will meet our demise in our chosen sinful path.

We know that the *"great fish"* was a whale because Jesus disclosed it in Matthew 12:40. The word *"swallow"* is also translated as "destroy" and "devour." The whale had every intention of eating and being satisfied and didn't gently swallow Jonah in order to preserve him.

Jonah was dead and entombed inside the whale's belly for three days and three nights. There is a constant debate about whether Jonah died, especially regarding how he could have prayed if he was dead. It is important to note that Jonah did die physically, otherwise, Matthew 12:40 would be false. Remember, Jonah was a proxy for Jesus. In mathematics, if A equals B, then B equals A. Jesus Christ died and was buried in a grave for three days and three nights. *Matthew 12:39 But he answered and said unto them, An evil and adulterous generation seeketh after a sign; and there shall no sign be given to it, but the sign of the prophet Jonas: [40] For as Jonas was three days and three nights in the whale's belly; so shall the Son of man be three days and three nights in the heart of the earth. [41]*

The men of Nineveh shall rise in judgment with this generation, and shall condemn it: because they repented at the preaching of Jonas; and, behold, a greater than Jonas is here.

The sign of death, burial, and resurrection is the most important sign that Jews and Gentiles need to believe in Jesus as the Christ, the Son of God from heaven.

Jonah chapter 1 ends with the death of the unrepentant prophet, just as all unrepentant sinners will eventually face death by sin and be dead in sin. Until they repent and accept Jesus Christ as Lord and Savior, they remain spiritually dead and can be considered the walking dead. ***Romans 6:23*** *For the wages of sin is death; but the gift of God is eternal life through Jesus Christ our Lord.*

Spiritual death, caused by sin, results in separation from God. While the physical body is temporary, the soul is eternal. When the physical body dies, the soul that is not cleansed of sin is also dead and is eternally separated from God. ***Ezekiel 18:4*** *Behold, all souls are mine; as the soul of the father, so also the soul of the son is mine: the soul that sinneth, it shall die.* ***John 8:12*** *Then spake Jesus again unto them, saying, I am the light of the world: he that followeth me shall not walk in darkness, but shall have the light of life. John 1:1 In the beginning was the Word, and the Word was with God, and the Word was God. ² The same was in the beginning with God. ³ All things were made by him; and without him was not any thing made that was made. ⁴ In him was life; and the life was the light of men.* ***1John 5:12*** *He that hath the Son hath life; and he that hath not the Son of God hath not life. ¹³ These things have I written unto you that believe on the name of the Son of God; that ye may know that ye have eternal life, and that ye may believe on the name of the Son of God.*

The Bible mentions a second death. How can someone who is already dead die again? (On the other hand, how can one be born again when the person has already been born once? Read John 3:1-

21.) The first death is the death of the body, and the second death is the death of the soul. ***Revelation 20:11*** *And I saw a great white throne, and him that sat on it, from whose face the earth and the heaven fled away; and there was found no place for them.* [12] *And I saw the dead, small and great, stand before God; and the books were opened: and another book was opened, which is the book of life: and the dead were judged out of those things which were written in the books, according to their works.* [13] *And the sea gave up the dead which were in it; and death and hell delivered up the dead which were in them: and they were judged every man according to their works.* [14] *And death and hell were cast into the lake of fire. This is the second death.*

A person who is born only once (physically) will die twice (physically and spiritually). A person who is born twice (physically and spiritually) will die only once (physically), and their soul will be saved.

Remember how Adam and Eve were immediately separated from God after they sinned, even though Adam lived for 930 years in the flesh? One doesn't have to die to start experiencing the consequences of being separated from God. Adam's afflictions began as soon as he was cast out of the Garden of Eden. Afflictions can come in many forms, including emptiness, depression, sickness, or in Jonah's case, death by fish.

There is nothing we can do to save ourselves from our sins. No amount of good works can erase our sins. That is why God, who so loved the world and did not want anyone to perish, but wanted all to come to repentance, gave His only begotten Son to die on the cross for our sins. By accepting Jesus Christ as Lord and Savior by faith, we can now have eternal life. Read John 3:16, Ephesians 2:8-9, Romans 10:9-10, 13, and listen to the hymn "Only Trust Him" by John Stockton.

Jonah 2:1 Then Jonah prayed unto the LORD his God out of the fish's belly,

Jonah didn't pray while he was running away from God, and it's likely that he also didn't pray when the shipmaster woke him up and said, *"Arise, call upon thy God"* in Jonah 1:6. However, we find him praying after spending three days and nights in captivity, which spawns debates. How could Jonah pray if he was dead? Remember that the soul of the dead rich man in Luke 16:19-31 cried to Abraham while in hell? Is it possible that Jonah died and his soul prayed to God from the fish's belly? Or that he died and came back to life on the third day and prayed? Regardless, God miraculously preserved him.

Three factors drove Jonah to prayer:

1. He was captive with no escape, as God had apprehended and incarcerated him.

2. He was afflicted, as the fish's belly was not the Tarshish he had imagined.

3. He was in a stinky place, similar to the prodigal son in Luke 15 who was humbled to the point of eating swine food and came to his senses. This led Jonah to realize that Nineveh was a better deal.

The story of Jonah in the fish's belly also represents the nation of Israel in captivity. Due to Israel's rebellion, the Assyrians captured the Northern Kingdom of Israel and the Babylonians captured the Southern Kingdom of Judah. However, while in captivity, Israel cried out to God, and He delivered them. ***Psalm 106:41 And he gave them into the hand of the heathen; and they that hated them ruled over them. 42 Their enemies also oppressed them, and they were brought into subjection under their hand. 43 Many times did he deliver them; but they provoked him with their*** *counsel, and were brought low for their iniquity.* Unfortunately, Israel continues to rebel even today, and my heart goes out to the Jews, as I know that they will face even more discipline. They will be deceived and persecuted by someone far worse than Hitler. This is described in Daniel 9:20-27 and Matthew 24:15-31.

All sinners will find themselves in a "fish belly," or the captivity of sin. This ranges from the law of sin (Romans 7:23) to the snare of the devil (2Timothy 2:26) to a physical prison cell. Prisoners should realize they are Jonah in a fish's belly—incarcerated, afflicted, and in a "stinky" place.

While it is not good to end up in the captivity of sin, it is important to recognize it. This recognition should drive us to prayer and make us ask how many afflictions we must suffer before we cry out to God and repent. Jonah 2:1 is the turning point, but unfortunately, many sinners remain stuck in Jonah 1:17, dead in sin. Affliction can be a good thing if it drives people to prayer and repentance.

Only Jesus Christ can free sinners from the captivity of sin. *Luke 4:18 The Spirit of the Lord is upon me, because he hath anointed me to preach the gospel to the poor; he hath sent me to heal the brokenhearted, to preach deliverance to the captives, and recovering of sight to the blind, to set at liberty them that are bruised, 19 To preach the acceptable year of the Lord.*

There is no freedom in sin, but there is true freedom in Christ. *John 8:34 Jesus answered them, Verily, verily, I say unto you, Whosoever committeth sin is the servant of sin. Romans 8:1 There is therefore now no condemnation to them which are in Christ Jesus, who walk not after the flesh, but after the Spirit. 2 For the law of the Spirit of life in Christ Jesus hath made me free from the law of sin and death. John 8:36 If the Son therefore shall make you free, ye shall be free indeed. Galatians 5:1 Stand fast therefore in the liberty wherewith Christ hath made us free, and be not entangled again with the yoke of bondage.*

Jonah 2:2 And said, I cried by reason of mine affliction unto the LORD, and he heard me; out of the belly of hell cried I, and thou heardest my voice.

Jonah cried to God out of his affliction. In distress, it is good to call upon the Lord. He is tender-hearted toward His children. **Psalm 18:6** *In my distress I called upon the LORD, and cried unto my God: he heard my voice out of his temple, and my cry came before him, even into his ears.* **Psalm 22:24** *For he hath not despised nor abhorred the affliction of the afflicted; neither hath he hid his face from him; but when he cried unto him, he heard.*

Jonah's prayer, recorded in Jonah 2:3-7, showcases God's mercy and kindness. Despite not acknowledging his sin or reflecting on his disobedience that caused the affliction, Jonah's prayer testifies to God's grace. Compare Jonah's prayer to David's: **Psalm 51:3** *For I acknowledge my transgressions: and my sin is ever before me.* *⁴ Against thee, thee only, have I sinned, and done this evil in thy sight: that thou mightest be justified when thou speakest, and be clear when thou judgest.*

Jonah's prayer was as if he suffered unjustly, which may appear off-putting at first until we recall that he was a proxy for Jesus, who truly suffered unjustly.

Jonah cried out to the Father, who heard his prayer. This is another example of Jonah being a type of Christ, as Jesus also prayed to the Father while He was suffering. In times of affliction, it's crucial to call out to a God who has ears to hear. **Psalm 77:1** *I cried unto God with my voice, even unto God with my voice; and he gave ear unto me.*

What is the point of calling upon a dead god? A dead god, whose bones are buried in the grave, cannot do anything for anyone. In contrast, Jesus Christ rose from the dead and is alive today. Sadly, my neighbor who is fighting a serious case of cancer is calling upon Buddha, who remains dead. **Psalm 115:3** *But our God is in the heavens: he hath done whatsoever he hath pleased. ⁴ Their idols are silver and gold, the work of men's hands. ⁵ They have mouths, but they speak not: eyes have they, but they see not: ⁶ They*

have ears, but they hear not: noses have they, but they smell not: ⁷
They have hands, but they handle not: feet have they, but they walk
not: neither speak they through their throat. ⁸ They that make them
are like unto them; so is every one that trusteth in them.

Prophetically, Jonah's affliction represents Israel in the
Great Tribulation period, which is prophesied throughout the Bible
from Genesis to Revelation. The message can be as subtle as the
story of Cain and Abel or as explicit as the books of Esther, Job,
Psalms, and the major and minor prophets. However, the Jews have
missed this message because they rejected Jesus Christ as their
Messiah, resulting in their blindness to God's truth (Romans 11:25).
The Bible also uses phrases such as *"time of Jacob's trouble," "in*
trouble," "that day," "those days," "last time," and *"woman in*
travail" to refer to the Great Tribulation period.

Jonah 2:1 states that Jonah cried to God from the belly of
the fish, while Jonah 2:2 says he cried to God from the belly of hell.
Which is it? The belly of the fish can be seen as a grave, a dark and
lightless place, similar to hell. (Job 10:21-22, Jude 1:13) Severe
distress and afflictions can make people feel like they are in hell.
The good news is that there is no place too far or deep that God
cannot hear the prayers of His people. (However, those who reject
Christ as their Savior will end up in the real hell, where there is no
hope of being heard by God.) If we ever find ourselves in a difficult
situation and all helplines fail, we better have a prayer line. Like
Jonah, we may feel like we are calling from the *"belly of hell,"* but
God can still hear us. He is faithful. Hallelujah! **Psalm 31:22** *For I*
said in my haste, I am cut off from before thine eyes: nevertheless
thou heardest the voice of my supplications when I cried unto thee.
Listen to the hymn, "What a friend we have in Jesus" by Joseph
Scriven and Charles Converse.

Jonah 2:3 For thou hadst cast me into the deep, in the midst of the seas; and the floods compassed me about: all thy billows and thy waves passed over me.

Jonah shed light on his experience of affliction. God's judgment came at the worst possible moment. The patient God allowed Jonah to run until he was in the middle of the deep ocean, and then He brought on the storm. It's important to note that the storm didn't come while Jonah was in shallow waters where he could have swam to shore.

Jonah sank when he was thrown overboard. The waves were over his head and the currents prevented him from coming up for air. He identified with Psalm 42:7, which states, *"Deep calleth unto deep at the noise of thy waterspouts: all thy waves and thy billows are gone over me."* What David said metaphorically happened literally to Jonah.

God's dealings with unrepentant sinners are consistent. He allows their sins to take them to the deep end, while still offering grace for repentance. However, it's important to understand that just because the skies are still clear, it doesn't mean that God is not watching or has fallen asleep on the job. The storm of His wrath will eventually come, and wave after wave of affliction will roll over the person until they repent or until their time on earth is up.

Some people go through life constantly wondering why everything is going wrong. They are surrounded by a flood of troubles and wave after wave of negative events roll over them. They try to fix their problems with various solutions, including religion, but not through a personal relationship with Jesus Christ according to the Bible.

Jonah recognized that his affliction was a result of his disobedience to God. If we find ourselves overwhelmed by the waters of calamity, it's important to examine ourselves to understand the source of the affliction so that we can address it properly. Why are we suffering? Is there anything that we need to repent of? **Psalm 139:23** *Search me, O God, and know my heart: try me, and know my thoughts:* [24] *And see if there be any wicked way in me, and lead me in the way everlasting.*

Jonah 2:4 Then I said, I am cast out of thy sight; yet I will look again toward thy holy temple.

Is there anything worse than drowning? How about drowning and being forsaken by God? Jonah realized he had fallen out of favor with God and had been expelled from His presence. God no longer wanted to see him. In his despair, Jonah identified with Psalm 31:22, which states, *"For I said in my haste, I am cut off from before thine eyes: nevertheless thou heardest the voice of my supplications when I cried unto thee."*

As the Jews practiced praying towards God's temple (1Kings 8:38-53), Jonah spiritually looked towards the temple—*"Yet I will look again toward thy holy temple."* The word *"again"* highlights the fact that when Jonah was obedient to God, he figuratively faced the temple. However, since he had turned away from God, he needed to repent and turn back towards the temple once more.

I think that even my cats understand this principle. When they misbehave and cause chaos, I put them outside and shut the door. Instinctively, they know they are in trouble and sit at the doorstep staring at the door and meowing, hoping to see me through the glass. Each time, they are overjoyed when they see me, thinking they may be able to come back inside. **Psalm 123:1** *Unto thee lift I up mine eyes, O thou that dwellest in the heavens.* [2] *Behold, as the eyes of servants look unto the hand of their masters, and as the eyes of a maiden unto the hand of her mistress; so our eyes wait upon the LORD our God, until that he have mercy upon us.*

What a wonderful God we serve! He is longsuffering, merciful, gracious, and ready to forgive. *Isaiah 44:22 I have blotted out, as a thick cloud, thy transgressions, and, as a cloud, thy sins: return unto me; for I have redeemed thee. 2Chronicles 7:14 If my people, which are called by my name, shall humble themselves, and pray, and seek my face, and turn from their wicked ways; then will I hear from heaven, and will forgive their sin, and will heal their land.*

Jonah 2:5 The waters compassed me about, even to the soul: the depth closed me round about, the weeds were wrapped about my head.

This verse describes drowning and death, lending credibility to the view that Jonah physically died.

Jonah sank into the deep and was entangled in seaweed before the whale swallowed him. The seaweed wrapped around his head like chains, preventing him from surfacing for air. This is a picture of sinners being held by the chains of sin, drowned, and swallowed by death.

Seaweed needs light for photosynthesis. They typically inhabit the ocean floor down to about 300 feet, although some live at deeper depths, where the penetration of sunlight is weaker, around 600 feet. These depths are in the first of the five layers of the ocean, known as the Epipelagic or Photic zone (surface to 656 feet below). At these depths, the pressure would have soon knocked Jonah unconscious and killed him.

The seaweed that wrapped around Jonah's head is significant because it represents the crown of thorns on Jesus' head. *John 19:1 Then Pilate therefore took Jesus, and scourged him. 2 And the soldiers platted a crown of thorns, and put it on his head, and they put on him a purple robe.* Both Jonah and Jesus wore the shameful crown before their death.

Jonah experienced three types of trouble:

- Jonah 2:3 – Trouble in the flesh. He suffered the wrath of God in the sea. (Jesus Christ was severely beaten before His crucifixion. *John 19:1 Then Pilate therefore took Jesus, and scourged him. Isaiah 53:5 But he was wounded for our transgressions, he was bruised for our iniquities: the chastisement of our peace was upon him; and with his stripes we are healed. Psalms 129:3 The plowers plowed upon my back: they made long their furrows.*)

- Jonah 2:4-5 – Trouble in the soul. He was forsaken and separated from God. (Jesus Christ was also forsaken by God. *Matthew 27:46 And about the ninth hour Jesus cried with a loud voice, saying, Eli, Eli, lama sabachthani? that is to say, My God, my God, why hast thou forsaken me?*)

- Jonah 2:6 – Trouble in life. He died and was buried in a belly grave. (Jesus Christ died and was buried in a grave. *Matthew 27:57 When the even was come, there came a rich man of Arimathaea, named Joseph, who also himself was Jesus' disciple: 58 He went to Pilate, and begged the body of Jesus. Then Pilate commanded the body to be delivered. 59 And when Joseph had taken the body, he wrapped it in a clean linen cloth, 60 And laid it in his own new tomb, which he had hewn out in the rock: and he rolled a great stone to the door of the sepulchre, and departed.*)

Sin yields the same three types of trouble. It wreaks havoc on the body with pain, disease, and sickness. It brings unrest and emptiness to the soul. It also kills both the physical body and soul. The worst outcome is to spend eternity in hell, not just in the grave. Being dead is the least of the problems for sinners who die in sin.

Jonah 2:6 I went down to the bottoms of the mountains; the earth with her bars was about me for ever: yet hast thou brought up my life from corruption, O LORD my God.

After swallowing Jonah, the whale dove even deeper, taking him to the base of the mountains deep beneath the ocean.

Whales are skilled divers, as their bodies are designed to withstand significant changes in pressure. Their ribs are held together by flexible cartilage, allowing them to compress under pressure. Their lungs can also safely collapse, preventing them from rupturing. For instance, sperm whales are known to dive to depths of 6,000 feet or more in search of giant squid that live in the third layer of the ocean, the Bathypelagic or Midnight zone (between 3,000 and 12,000 feet below). The next layer is the Abyssopelagic or Abyss (between 13,000 and 20,000 feet below), which marks the start of the continental rise. The phrase *"the bottoms of the mountains"* could refer to the Abyss zone, as the deepest part of the Mediterranean Sea is 17,280 feet. The exact depth the whale took Jonah to is unknown, but it's safe to say that at these depths, Jonah would have been dead.

That was the lowest point in Jonah's life. All hope of returning to the land of the living and the land flowing with milk and honey was lost. He was banned from returning forever, and there was nothing he could do to escape God's decree concerning him. The whale's belly was his grave and seemingly the end of his story. **Psalm 88:5** *Free among the dead, like the slain that lie in the grave, whom thou rememberest no more: and they are cut off from thy hand. ⁶ Thou hast laid me in the lowest pit, in darkness, in the deeps. ⁷ Thy wrath lieth hard upon me, and thou hast afflicted me with all thy waves. Selah.*

Sin sinks and drowns people to a level beyond any chance of rescue, except through the Lord Jesus Christ. Sinners who die in their sins share a similar hopeless state. They will be in hell deep beneath the earth with no chance of returning to the land of the living forever. They all desire to escape, but none has the power to break free.

Thankfully, God heard Jonah's prayer and rescued him from corruption, or the pit of belly hell—*"yet hast thou brought up my life from corruption, O LORD my God."*

A sinner condemned to hell is set free. That's me. Jesus Christ has rescued my soul from corruption. ***Psalm 86:13*** *For great is thy mercy toward me: and thou hast delivered my soul from the lowest hell.* ***Isaiah 38:17*** *Behold, for peace I had great bitterness: but thou hast in love to my soul delivered it from the pit of corruption: for thou hast cast all my sins behind thy back.* If sin is weighing you down and you don't know Jesus Christ as Lord and Savior, accept Him into your heart today. See Appendix A.

Don't miss the gospel in Jonah 2:6. The phrase *"yet hast thou brought up my life from corruption"* is an unmistakable reference to Jesus Christ. It is a prophecy that Christ would not see corruption (or destruction) in the grave. This is yet another example of Jonah as a type of Christ. Just as God rescued Jonah from the belly grave, Christ rose from the grave to conquer sin and death. ***Psalm 16:10*** *For thou wilt not leave my soul in hell; neither wilt thou suffer thine Holy One to see corruption.* ***Acts 2:22*** *Ye men of Israel, hear these words; Jesus of Nazareth, a man approved of God among you by miracles and wonders and signs, which God did by him in the midst of you, as ye yourselves also know:* ^{23} *Him, being delivered by the determinate counsel and foreknowledge of God, ye have taken, and by wicked hands have crucified and slain:* ^{24} *Whom God hath raised up, having loosed the pains of death: because it was not possible that he should be holden of it.* ^{25} *For David speaketh concerning him, I foresaw the Lord always before my face, for he is on my right hand, that I should not be moved:* ^{26} *Therefore did my heart rejoice, and my tongue was glad; moreover also my flesh shall* rest in hope: *²⁷ Because thou wilt not leave my soul in hell, neither wilt thou suffer thine Holy One to see corruption. ²⁸ Thou hast made known to me the ways of life; thou shalt make me full of joy with thy countenance. ²⁹ Men and brethren, let me freely speak unto you of the patriarch David, that he is both dead and buried, and his sepulchre is with us unto this day. ³⁰ Therefore being a prophet, and knowing that God had sworn with an oath to him, that of the fruit of his loins, according to the flesh, he would raise up Christ to sit on his throne; ³¹ He seeing this before spake of the resurrection of Christ, that his soul was not left in hell, neither his flesh did see corruption.* Also read Acts 13:33-37.

Jonah 2:7 When my soul fainted within me I remembered the LORD: and my prayer came in unto thee, into thine holy temple. ⁸ They that observe lying vanities forsake their own mercy.

The chastisement of God upon Jonah was overwhelming, reaching his innermost soul and causing him to give up or faint as he was engulfed by troubles. His will to disobey was broken, and he felt as though he was expiring. **Psalm 32:4 For day and night thy hand was heavy upon me: my moisture is turned into the drought of summer. Selah.**

If you were in Jonah's shoes, who would you call for help? Interestingly, there are two groups of people, each calling a different helpline. One group calls on God, and the other calls on "lying vanities."

Jonah remembered God and thought of His power and mercy. So, Jonah turned to prayer. His prayer pierced through all barriers, reached God's sanctuary, and was heard. **Psalm 46:1 God is our refuge and strength, a very present help in trouble. ² Therefore will not we fear, though the earth be removed, and though the mountains be carried into the midst of the sea; ³ Though the waters** *thereof roar and be troubled, though the mountains shake with the swelling thereof. Selah.*

Some people call on *"lying vanities"* or worthless idols. This could range from an object to a dead god, or even a living person who is a sinner like themselves. None can save, but unfortunately, the way seems right to them. **Proverbs 14:12** *There is a way which seemeth right unto a man, but the end thereof are the ways of death.* These people forsake their own mercy, which is God's lovingkindness served on Calvary's cross. **John 3:16** *For God so loved the world, that he gave his only begotten Son, that whosoever believeth in him should not perish, but have everlasting life. ¹⁷ For God sent not his Son into the world to condemn the world; but that the world through him might be saved. ¹⁸ He that believeth on him is not condemned: but he that believeth not is condemned already, because he hath not believed in the name of the only begotten Son of God. ¹⁹ And this is the condemnation, that light is come into the world, and men loved darkness rather than light, because their deeds were evil.*

In life and death situations, it is important to call the right helpline and to remember that sin turns away the mercy of God. Wrath can be expected when people *"forsake their own mercy."* Talk about shooting oneself in the foot!

Prophetically, Israel will remember God in their darkest hour and call on Him nationally when the soul of their nation faints under the persecution of the antichrist.

Jonah 2:9 But I will sacrifice unto thee with the voice of thanksgiving; I will pay that that I have vowed. Salvation is of the LORD.

Jonah received God's mercy with thanksgiving. As an Old Testament prophet and Jew, it is interesting that Jonah simply thanked God for His salvation without atoning for his sins through the sacrifices and offerings prescribed by the Law of Moses. It was as if his death was enough. In this way, Jonah was a foreshadowing of Jesus, who offered his own body and blood as a perfect sin offering, thereby completely pacifying the wrath of God. As a result, animal sacrifices are no longer necessary. *Hebrews 10:1 For the law having a shadow of good things to come, and not the very image of the things, can never with those sacrifices which they offered year by year continually make the comers thereunto perfect. ⁴ For then would they not have ceased to be offered? because that the worshippers once purged should have had no more conscience of sins. ³ But in those sacrifices there is a remembrance again made of sins every year. ⁴ For it is not possible that the blood of bulls and of goats should take away sins. ⁵ Wherefore when he cometh into the world, he saith, Sacrifice and offering thou wouldest not, but a body hast thou prepared me: ⁶ In burnt offerings and sacrifices for sin thou hast had no pleasure. ⁷ Then said I, Lo, I come (in the volume of the book it is written of me,) to do thy will, O God. ⁸ Above when he said, Sacrifice and offering and burnt offerings and offering for sin thou wouldest not, neither hadst pleasure therein; which are offered by the law; ⁹ Then said he, Lo, I come to do thy will, O God. He taketh away the first, that he may establish the second. ¹⁰ By the which will we are sanctified through the offering of the body of Jesus Christ once for all.*

According to Jonah 2:9, every believer who is delivered from death should do four things:

1. Be different from the lost. *"But I..."* should be different from the foolish people who worship worthless idols. Proverbs 9:6 says, *"Forsake the foolish, and live; and go in the way of understanding."* We should live a godly and holy life that is different from the people on the broad way that leads to destruction. *Joshua 24:15 And if*

it seem evil unto you to serve the LORD, choose you this day whom ye will serve; whether the gods which your fathers served that were on the other side of the flood, or the gods of the Amorites, in whose land ye dwell: but as for me and my house, we will serve the LORD.

2. Be thankful for God's salvation. We can never thank Jesus enough for His salvation, which He dearly paid for with His life on Calvary's cross. We should continually express our gratitude for eternity, and it still wouldn't be enough.

3. Be fulfilling our vows to God. When we received Christ for the forgiveness of our sins, we made a transaction with God, essentially vowing to make Him the Lord of our lives and to serve Him.

4. Be witnessing. Salvation is of the Lord, and we should share the good news of God's salvation with others. ***Acts 4:10*** *Be it known unto you all, and to all the people of Israel, that by the name of Jesus Christ of Nazareth, whom ye crucified, whom God raised from the dead, even by him doth this man stand here before you whole.* *[11] This is the stone which was set at nought of you builders, which is become the head of the corner. [12] Neither is there salvation in any other: for there is none other name under heaven given among men, whereby we must be saved.*

Jonah 2:10 And the LORD spake unto the fish, and it vomited out Jonah upon the dry land.

Do you speak fish? God did. He commanded the whale to vomit Jonah up, and it obeyed Him. After three days of indigestion, the fish was probably glad to do so.

Just four verses prior, Jonah said, *"The earth with her bars was about me for ever."* He thought he would never return to the land of the living. But now, he was back on dry land. Imagine how he must have felt after his ordeal. Even though he stunk like fish vomit, I don't think he minded at all.

Jonah's release from captivity is a picture of Israel's future deliverance from the antichrist. ***Psalms 126:1*** *When the LORD turned again the captivity of Zion, we were like them that dream. ² Then was our mouth filled with laughter, and our tongue with singing: then said they among the heathen, The LORD hath done great things for them. ³ The LORD hath done great things for us; whereof we are glad.*

4 – From Salvation to Service

How can we top the incredible resurrection of a disobedient and dead prophet who spent three days and nights in a whale's belly? How about the repentance and salvation of a wicked Gentile nation?

Having been delivered from death, Jonah returned to his service to God. Now humbled, he ventured to Nineveh and delivered God's proclamation to the people he despised. The result was astounding: the entire wicked Gentile nation repented of their sins.

Repentance and salvation are the hallmarks of Jonah 3. The chapter can be outlined as follows:

- The repentance of God's servant – Jonah 3:1-4
- The repentance of God's enemies – Jonah 3:5-10

Jonah 3:1 And the word of the LORD came unto Jonah the second time, saying, ² Arise, go unto Nineveh, that great city, and preach unto it the preaching that I bid thee.

In His mercy and patience, God recommissioned Jonah to deliver His message in Nineveh, as He told him in Jonah 1:2. This time, Jonah obeyed.

We may derail in our relationship with God, but it is good to know that He is still interested in our service when we repent.

Having just been through the wringer, Jonah was probably happy to obey God. Speaking of the wringer, sometimes we see people suffer from their bad decisions, and we tend to try to smooth over the consequences without thinking it through, especially when it comes to our loved ones. While helping is generally a good thing to do, we should keep in mind that we may be hurting people by short-circuiting God's course of discipline, which aims to yield obedience. Wisdom is called for. Sometimes the best thing to do is to let people experience God's chastisement to the fullest. This "tough love" is not a popular position in our society nowadays. It makes those who take this stance look heartless, while the helpers look good. Ironically, benevolence makes good publicity at the cost of the sufferers by denying them the chance to learn from their bad decisions. Consequently, these wayward individuals become repeat offenders. We should recognize that God does not punish people for the sake of punishment but to draw them to Him so that He can bless them.

Do you think God's discipline of Jonah was too harsh? Would you have thrown him a lifeline when he was overboard? Can you bear to watch a man suffer the consequences of his bad decisions and do nothing? Do you think God's discipline of the Jewish prodigal son in Luke 15 was excessive when He made him eat swine food? Would you have provided him with kosher food? Do you think God's judgment on Israel for rejecting Jesus Christ and failing to be a light to the Gentiles was too severe when He allowed Nazi Germany to commit genocide on millions of Jews during the Holocaust? And to consider that God's judgment is not over yet. In the future, most Jews will be killed by the antichrist. If Israel was a tree, only a stump would remain. The Bible prophesies that this is what it will take before Israel will be right with God. *Isaiah 1:9 Except the LORD of hosts had left unto us a very small remnant, we should have been as Sodom, and we should have been like unto Gomorrah. Isaiah 10:20 And it shall come to pass in that day, that the remnant of Israel, and such as are escaped of the house of*

Jacob, shall no more again stay upon him that smote them; but shall stay upon the LORD, the Holy One of Israel, in truth. ²¹ *The remnant shall return, even the remnant of Jacob, unto the mighty God. ²² For though thy people Israel be as the sand of the sea, yet a remnant of them shall return: the consumption decreed shall overflow with righteousness. ²³ For the Lord GOD of hosts shall make a consumption, even determined, in the midst of all the land.*

Finally, do you think God's wrath on His beloved Son was excessive when He placed the sins of the world upon Him and allowed Him to die a horrific death on the cross? One important lesson that many people fail to learn is that obedience comes through suffering. Even Jesus Christ had to learn obedience through His suffering. **Hebrew 5:8** *Though he were a Son, yet learned he obedience by the things which he suffered; ⁹ And being made perfect, he became the author of eternal salvation unto all them that obey him.* It is scary to imagine what kind of wringer God may have to put us through to be right with Him.

Jonah 3:3 So Jonah arose, and went unto Nineveh, according to the word of the LORD. Now Nineveh was an exceeding great city of three days' journey. ⁴ And Jonah began to enter into the city a day's journey, and he cried, and said, Yet forty days, and Nineveh shall be overthrown.

Jonah is now aligned with God. He went to Nineveh as God commanded, delivering a straightforward 8-word message of judgment. Prophetically, this represents Israel repenting and being willing to fulfill its duty to the Gentile nations. (See Isaiah 49:6, Acts 13:47)

Jonah was given a specific assignment that demanded his obedience. It is difficult to comprehend the cost he paid for initially rejecting such a simple task. Similarly, God has given us the simple task of sharing the gospel with those who are lost. Why don't we do it as frequently as we should?

Nineveh was an extremely large city by biblical standards. Jonah traveled into the city for a day's journey (approximately 20 miles) and began preaching on the streets. This type of preaching was unlike what we typically imagine. It was more like dropping and detonating a doomsday message.

This one-day penetration into Nineveh is intriguing. As the city was a three-day journey in total, it would have taken two more days to reach the opposite side. In Jonah 4:5, Jonah crossed the city and was on the east side. These two glimpses of Jonah in Nineveh depict the two comings of Jesus Christ. He appeared to the Jews during His first coming, which corresponds to Jonah's first day in Nineveh. Jesus will come again two thousand years later. (The Bible says one day is with the Lord as a thousand years [2Peter 3:8], so the remaining two days are as two thousand years.) This is year 2021 A.D. Jesus is coming soon!

Just as Jonah reappeared on the east side of Nineveh, Jesus will reappear on the east side of Jerusalem. *Zechariah 14:4 And his feet shall stand in that day upon the mount of Olives, which is before Jerusalem on the east, and the mount of Olives shall cleave in the midst thereof toward the east and toward the west, and there shall be a very great valley; and half of the mountain shall remove toward the north, and half of it toward the south.*

Just as Jonah preached repentance, Jesus did too. *Matthew 4:17 From that time Jesus began to preach, and to say, Repent: for the kingdom of heaven is at hand.*

Interestingly, the Ninevites did not harass Jonah. They could have questioned his audacity, asking, "Who does this weak Jew think he is to preach God's judgment to us? Didn't we conquer his nation and enslave his people? How can this lone individual possibly overthrow our great city in 40 days?" However, from Jonah's perspective, he did not care if he died. He preferred that his enemies not repent and face God's judgment.

God's word was powerful and effective, as seen in the next verses. **Hebrews 4:12** *For the word of God is quick, and powerful, and sharper than any twoedged sword, piercing even to the dividing asunder of soul and spirit, and of the joints and marrow, and is a discerner of the thoughts and intents of the heart.* **Isaiah 55:11** *So shall my word be that goeth forth out of my mouth: it shall not return unto me void, but it shall accomplish that which I please, and it shall prosper in the thing whereto I sent it.*

The one-sentence message of judgment was impactful. It started with a grace period of 40 days, followed by judgment that would devastate the city. God's plan was set in motion and time was running out, with repentance being the only way to prevent it. (In the Bible, the number 40 symbolizes a time of testing, a period when God tests a person or nation.)

The same judgment awaits every individual. Hebrews 9:27 states, *"And as it is appointed unto men once to die, but after this the judgment."* We have this lifetime to repent of our sins, or we will face the consequences. There is no guarantee of tomorrow, so let us accept Jesus Christ as our Lord and Savior, receive the forgiveness of our sins, and serve Him before it is too late. **James 4:14** *Whereas ye know not what shall be on the morrow. For what is your life? It is even a vapour, that appeareth for a little time, and then vanisheth away.*

Jonah 3:5 So the people of Nineveh believed God, and proclaimed a fast, and put on sackcloth, from the greatest of them even to the least of them.

The exact location where the whale vomited Jonah is unknown. If it was on a beach in Joppa, he would have had to undertake a long journey of over 500 miles to reach Nineveh. People along the way would have learned of and spread news of his incredible and harrowing experience.

When Jonah arrived in Nineveh, it did not take much effort to persuade the Ninevites to repent of their sins. They saw a prophet who had gone to "hell" for disobeying God's commandment, and returned to the land of the living after repenting. (Luke 11:30 states that Jonah was a sign to the Ninevites.) The Ninevites were frightened by God's message concerning their nation and recognized that this God was not to be trifled with. When the verse says, *"the people of Nineveh believed God,"* they took His words seriously, believed them, and repented of their sins.

The straightforward message of judgment caused the Ninevites to repent. A few decades ago, preachers delivered messages referred to as "fire and brimstone." Many sinners turned away from their sins and turned to Jesus Christ. Today, this type of message is highly unpopular, as people prefer to hear about the soft and loving side of God while retaining their sins. These people are aware that there are two sides to every coin, but choose to keep their eyes closed to the side of judgment. It should be known that the loving God is also the King of wrath. It is essential to be in a right relationship with God, which starts with a personal relationship with His Son, Jesus Christ.

It is important to note that salvation starts with faith in God's word. *"So the people of Nineveh believed God,"* followed by their act of repentance (Jonah 3:6-8). The Ninevites' faith in God's word was counted to them for righteousness, just as Abraham's faith in God was counted to him for righteousness. (Romans 4:3, Galatians 3:6, James 2:23)

The Ninevites were Gentiles and did not have to observe the Jewish tradition of wearing sackcloth, but they chose to do so perhaps because the messenger was a Jew. In biblical times, Jews wore sackcloth for various reasons, including mourning the dead (Genesis 37:34, 2Samuel 3:31, 2Samuel 21:10), expressing humility (1Kings 21:27-29), expressing distress (2Kings 6:30, 2Kings 19:1, Esther 4:1, 3, Job 16:15), and repenting of sin (1Chronicles 21:16, Nehemiah 9:1, Matthew 11:21). A good example can be found in Daniel 9, where Daniel understood the prophecy of Jeremiah regarding God's judgment on Jerusalem, its desolation, and the 70 years of captivity in Babylon. See how Daniel reacted to this understanding, confessing his own sins and the sins of his nation to God.

It is fascinating that this was a national repentance, from *"the greatest of them even to the least of them"* at a time of great power and wealth. Typically, people would be proud and arrogant, with no need for God. Can you think of any other country that has humbled itself and repented before God? Can your family or church do the same?

Instead of wearing sackcloth, God desires for His children to be clothed with humility. This is demonstrated through submission to God's word and to one another. *1Peter 5:5 Likewise, ye younger, submit yourselves unto the elder. Yea, all of you be subject one to another, and be clothed with humility: for God resisteth the proud, and giveth grace to the humble.*

What is important to God is not just the appearance of humility, but honesty in one's innermost being and a heart that is broken and contrite. *Isaiah 58:5 Is it such a fast that I have chosen? a day for a man to afflict his soul? is it to bow down his head as a bulrush, and to spread sackcloth and ashes under him? wilt thou call this a fast, and an acceptable day to the LORD? [6] Is not this the fast that I have chosen? to loose the bands of wickedness, to undo the heavy burdens, and to let the oppressed go free, and that ye break every yoke? [7] Is it not to deal thy bread to the hungry, and that thou bring the poor that are cast out to thy house? when thou seest the naked, that thou cover him; and that thou hide not thyself from thine own flesh?* **Psalms 51:17** *The sacrifices of God are a broken spirit: a broken and a contrite heart, O God, thou wilt not despise.*

Even though the Ninevites were oppressors, there was a deeper reason for their sinful behavior. Solomon recognized that the solution to oppression is the Comforter, the Holy Spirit of God, who can be received by accepting Jesus Christ as Lord and Savior. **Ecclesiastes 4:1** *So I returned, and considered all the oppressions that are done under the sun: and behold the tears of such as were oppressed, and they had no comforter; and on the side of their oppressors there was power; but they had no comforter.* **John 14:16** *And I will pray the Father, and he shall give you another Comforter, that he may abide with you for ever;* *17* *Even the Spirit of truth; whom the world cannot receive, because it seeth him not, neither knoweth him: but ye know him; for he dwelleth with you, and shall be in you.* *18* *I will not leave you comfortless: I will come to you.*

Below are four important points to consider:

1. God loves sinners and desires to bless them instead of punishing them.

2. The worst of sinners are often aware of their wrongdoing, and their conscience convicts them. Many are open to repenting when they hear God's message.

3. Sharing the gospel is the responsibility of all who have been resurrected in Christ. If you have experienced the new birth, you too have been raised with Christ and are empowered to share the gospel message. There is nothing like a living dead with nothing to lose and a simple gospel message. **Colossians 2:12** *Buried with him in baptism, wherein also ye are risen with him through the faith of the operation of God, who hath raised him from the dead.* **Romans 6:3** *Know ye not, that so many*

of us as were baptized into Jesus Christ were baptized into his death? [4] Therefore we are buried with him by baptism into death: that like as Christ was raised up from the dead by the glory of the Father, even so we also should walk in newness of life. [5] For if we have been planted together in the likeness of his death, we shall be also in the likeness of his resurrection.

4. Your repentance and obedience can bring salvation to others. Consider the example of Jonah, whose repentance led to the salvation of many souls.

Jonah 3:6 For word came unto the king of Nineveh, and he arose from his throne, and he laid his robe from him, and covered him with sackcloth, and sat in ashes.

God's warning of impending judgment echoed like a bomb throughout the highest office in Nineveh. The fierce king of Nineveh was impacted by the message and believed it. To his credit, he led by example, humbling himself before calling on others to do the same.

Humility is pleasing to the Lord. As a result, the king of Nineveh was granted unmerited favor, which is known as grace. ***James 4:6b*** *God resisteth the proud, but giveth grace unto the humble.* ***James 4:8*** *Draw nigh to God, and he will draw nigh to you. Cleanse your hands, ye sinners; and purify your hearts, ye double minded. [9] Be afflicted, and mourn, and weep: let your laughter be turned to mourning, and your joy to heaviness. [10] Humble yourselves in the sight of the Lord, and he shall lift you up.*

Jonah 3:7 And he caused it to be proclaimed and published through Nineveh by the decree of the king and his nobles, saying,

Let neither man nor beast, herd nor flock, taste any thing: let them not feed, nor drink water: ⁸ But let man and beast be covered with sackcloth, and cry mightily unto God: yea, let them turn every one from his evil way, and from the violence that is in their hands. ⁹ Who can tell if God will turn and repent, and turn away from his fierce anger, that we perish not?

The king of Nineveh proclaimed God's judgment throughout his kingdom and ordered his people to show their remorse by fasting and wearing sackcloth. He also instructed them to cry out to God for mercy and to repent of their evil ways. As a further expression of their contrition, they were to remove all decorations and ornaments from their animals, such as horses and camels, which were used for pleasure or business, and cover them with sackcloth as well. *Ezra 8:21 Then I proclaimed a fast there, at the river of Ahava, that we might afflict ourselves before our God, to seek of him a right way for us, and for our little ones, and for all our substance.*

The phrase *"cry mightily unto God: yea, let them turn every one from his evil way, and from the violence that is in their hands"* is a representation of true repentance. Unfortunately, many people mock God by crying out to Him about their problems, but refuse to repent of their sins.

The Ninevites were known to be evil and barbaric. Nahum 3:1 describes Nineveh as a "bloody city." They were murderers, liars, and untrustworthy, often engaging in robbery. They were also filled with idolatry, promiscuity, and witchcraft. God had grown tired of their sins. *Nahum 3:1 Woe to the bloody city! it is all full of lies and robbery; the prey departeth not; ² The noise of a whip, and the noise of the rattling of the wheels, and of the pransing horses, and of the jumping chariots. ³ The horseman lifteth up both the bright sword and the glittering spear: and there is a multitude of slain, and a great number of carcases; and there is none end of their corpses; they stumble upon their corpses: ⁴ Because of the multitude of the whoredoms of the wellfavoured harlot, the mistress of witchcrafts, that selleth nations through her whoredoms, and families through her witchcrafts. ⁵ Behold, I am against thee, saith the LORD of hosts; and I will discover thy skirts upon thy face, and I will shew the nations thy nakedness, and the kingdoms thy shame. ⁶ And I will cast abominable filth upon thee, and make thee vile, and will set thee as a gazingstock. ⁷ And it shall come to pass, that all they that look upon thee shall flee from thee, and say, Nineveh is laid waste: who will bemoan her? whence shall I seek comforters for thee?*

The king of Nineveh had two options: to harden himself in his sins and face God's wrath, or to repent and seek mercy in the hopes of being saved. What would you have done if you were in his position?

Despite their wicked ways, God loved the Ninevites and offered them a gracious deal. If they repented of their sins, He would forgive them and retract His judgment. This may seem unbelievable given all the evil the Ninevites had committed, but it is true.

God offers us the same gracious deal. If we confess our sins and receive Jesus Christ as Lord and Savior by faith, He will forgive all of our transgressions. It would be foolish to pass up such a generous offer. **Romans 10:9** *That if thou shalt confess with thy mouth the Lord Jesus, and shalt believe in thine heart that God hath raised him from the dead, thou shalt be saved. ¹⁰ For with the heart man believeth unto righteousness; and with the mouth confession is made unto salvation.*

Jonah 3:10 And God saw their works, that they turned from their evil way; and God repented of the evil, that he had said that he would do unto them; and he did it not.

The Ninevites repented upon hearing God's words. When people take God's words seriously and repent, they are spared from His righteous judgment. *Job 33:27 He looketh upon men, and if any say, I have sinned, and perverted that which was right, and it profited me not; 28 He will deliver his soul from going into the pit, and his life shall see the light. Jeremiah 18:7 At what instant I shall speak concerning a nation, and concerning a kingdom, to pluck up, and to pull down, and to destroy it; 8 If that nation, against whom I have pronounced, turn from their evil, I will repent of the evil that I thought to do unto them.*

God sees everyone's actions, whether they are good or bad, and nothing is hidden from Him. Seven times in the book of Revelation, God says, *"I know thy works."* The proof of repentance is not in words, but in actions. However, this does not mean showing humility by wearing sackcloth and ashes or fasting, but rather, turning away from evil and turning towards God, which starts in the heart after receiving God's words.

Jesus praised the Ninevites in the gospels. *Matthew 12:41 The men of Nineveh shall rise in judgment with this generation, and shall condemn it: because they repented at the preaching of Jonas; and, behold, a greater than Jonas is here.* Despite having only one prophet who performed no miracles and a 40-day grace period, they repented immediately. In contrast, the Jews had many prophets, signs, miracles, years of grace, and even the Messiah Himself, yet remained unrepentant. The people of Sodom and Gomorrah will face a more tolerable judgment than these Jews.

Through Jonah's death and resurrection, a nation was saved. Through the death and resurrection of Jesus Christ, a world of believers is saved.

5 – A Pathetic Prophet Afterall

It's amazing that such a flawed prophet of God as Jonah could be so fruitful for Him. God is great and can use our weaknesses for His glory. His word is powerful and works effectively in those who believe (1Thessalonians 2:13).

The conclusion of the book of Jonah includes a dialogue between God and the penman. Jonah remained a hateful person, still wishing retribution on his enemies. He was angry at God for showing mercy to the Ninevites. God gently reproved him.

Jonah, like some of us, was a disciple in the making with rough edges that God worked on over time. Notice how incredibly patient and kind God was towards him. This should give us hope that God will help us in our walk with Him, which is a process, and that our best days and the final product are still ahead of us.

The outline of Jonah 4 can be as follows:

1. A displeased prophet – Jonah 4:1-4.
2. A spectator prophet – Jonah 4:5.
3. A learning prophet – Jonah 4:6-11

Jonah 4:1 But it displeased Jonah exceedingly, and he was very angry. ² And he prayed unto the LORD, and said, I pray thee, O LORD, was not this my saying, when I was yet in my country? Therefore I fled before unto Tarshish: for I knew that thou art a gracious God, and merciful, slow to anger, and of great kindness, and repentest thee of the evil. ³ Therefore now, O LORD, take, I beseech thee, my life from me; for it is better for me to die than to live. ⁴ Then said the LORD, Doest thou well to be angry?

According to Luke 15:7, heaven rejoices over one sinner who repents. Imagine the celebration they had in heaven when the Ninevites repented. But Jonah refused to be joyful about the success of God's word. Instead, he was displeased and angry with God for sparing the Ninevites.

How quickly Jonah went from rejoicing over his own salvation to complaining. After God delivered him from the belly of the whale, he said, *"But I will sacrifice unto thee with the voice of thanksgiving; I will pay that that I have vowed. Salvation is of the LORD."* (Jonah 2:9) Having received an extraordinary measure of mercy after disobeying God, he was now upset that the Ninevites did the right thing. Jonah knew that God is kind to those who repent. So, to prevent his enemies from experiencing God's pardoning mercy, he refused to preach to the Ninevites and instead fled to Tarshish. Jonah was not afraid of death, but his worst fear was the salvation of his enemies.

Jonah had such a deep-seated hatred for the Assyrians that he would rather die than see them live and be at peace with God. He could not get rid of the root of bitterness in his heart. However, God is patient with sinners and does not want any of them to perish, but wants all to come to repentance. (2Peter 3:9)

God could have fulfilled Jonah's death wish and killed him instantly, but He was gentle and understanding, willing to reason with him. It was as if God said, "I understand how you feel about these people who have hurt you, but you need to look at this from My kingdom perspective. You wish for them to go to hell, but I wish for them to have life." Yet, God questioned Jonah's attitude, *"Doest thou well to be angry?"* The question struck Jonah at the core of his conscience. He had no answer because he knew his reaction to the success of God's mission was absurd.

This demonstration of God's wisdom should be in every anger management course—*"Doest thou well to be angry?"* When our hearts and minds are filled with anger, we should condition ourselves to check: Is it good for me to be angry, angry all the time, and angry for a long time? And, is it good for me to be angry or despise wicked people who receive God's mercy? Are there people so wicked that God will not pardon if they repent? *Ephesians 4:26 Be ye angry, and sin not: let not the sun go down upon your wrath: ²⁷ Neither give place to the devil.*

Another lesson we can take from this passage of scripture is that we cannot serve God on our own terms. Jonah had no problem serving God in his own country, but struggled as a messenger to his enemies. We must have a kingdom mindset and have the Father's business at heart.

We must also get rid of any root of bitterness in our hearts. If we hate certain people, God has a great sense of humor; we may end up ministering to them. I always laugh when I hear the song "Please Don't Send Me to Africa" by Scott Westley Brown. The YouTube video is funny.

Jonah 4:5 So Jonah went out of the city, and sat on the east side of the city, and there made him a booth, and sat under it in the shadow, till he might see what would become of the city.

Unable to answer God's question, Jonah ventured to the east side of the city and found a spot to observe from. He built a shelter to take refuge from the heat and planned to watch the outcome of the 40-day grace period. He might have hoped for some form of judgment to still come down.

Why didn't Jonah stay at someone's home? One would expect that, given the Ninevites' acceptance of his message, he would have received multiple invitations for food and lodging.

Matthew 10:14 says, *"And whosoever shall not receive you, nor hear your words, when ye depart out of that house or city, shake off the dust of your feet."* But this was a good outcome. Jonah would have been welcomed into the homes of nobles. Who wouldn't want to have God's prophet in their home for extra insurance? It's possible that Jonah did receive invitations, but didn't want to be in the crosshairs of judgment if it came.

A good servant of God would have continued to preach His message and tried to save as many people as possible from judgment. Unfortunately, Jonah only preached once and then retired to his shelter. We should never retire from serving the Lord.

The second appearance of Jonah in east Nineveh is an interesting picture of Christ's second coming, as previously discussed in Jonah 3:4 above.

Jonah 4:6 And the LORD God prepared a gourd, and made it to come up over Jonah, that it might be a shadow over his head, to deliver him from his grief. So Jonah was exceeding glad of the gourd.

Jonah sat in his stall, miserable over the repentance of the Ninevites and exposed to the weather. It was like watching his favorite sports team lose while baking in the hot sun. His makeshift shelter didn't provide adequate protection from the cold night or the heat of the day.

God continued His lovingkindness toward Jonah and miraculously grew a gourd plant to shade him from the sun and ease his sorrow. (The type of gourd plant is unknown, but some believe it was the Castor bean plant, which has broad leaves and can grow up to 10 feet tall.) Jonah loved this plant and went from being exceedingly displeased (Jonah 4:1) to being exceedingly glad. Talk about a rapid mood change.

However, Jonah was glad for the plant but did not acknowledge or praise God for the provision. This spelled trouble for him in the following verses.

This verse also has a prophetic significance, foreshadowing Israel in the end times. The word *"shadow"* here refers to trust or protection. As seen in Judges 9:15, *"And the bramble said unto the trees, If in truth ye anoint me king over you, then come and put your trust in my shadow: and if not, let fire come out of the bramble, and devour the cedars of Lebanon."* In the end times, Israel will rely on its own power and resources for protection, just as Jonah relied on his makeshift stall. But this self-reliance will prove inadequate and leave Israel miserable. However, God will keep His promises to Abraham, Isaac, and Jacob and miraculously deliver Israel from its sorrow, bringing them great joy when they see Jesus Christ, the Messiah, coming to their rescue.

This passage also teaches us an important principle: we should find our happiness in God and not in worldly things. Even though Jonah was joyful for God's provision, he didn't find true happiness in the shelter he built for himself.

Jonah 4:7 But God prepared a worm when the morning rose the next day, and it smote the gourd that it withered. ⁸ And it came to pass, when the sun did arise, that God prepared a vehement east wind; and the sun beat upon the head of Jonah, that he fainted, and wished in himself to die, and said, It is better for me to die than to live.

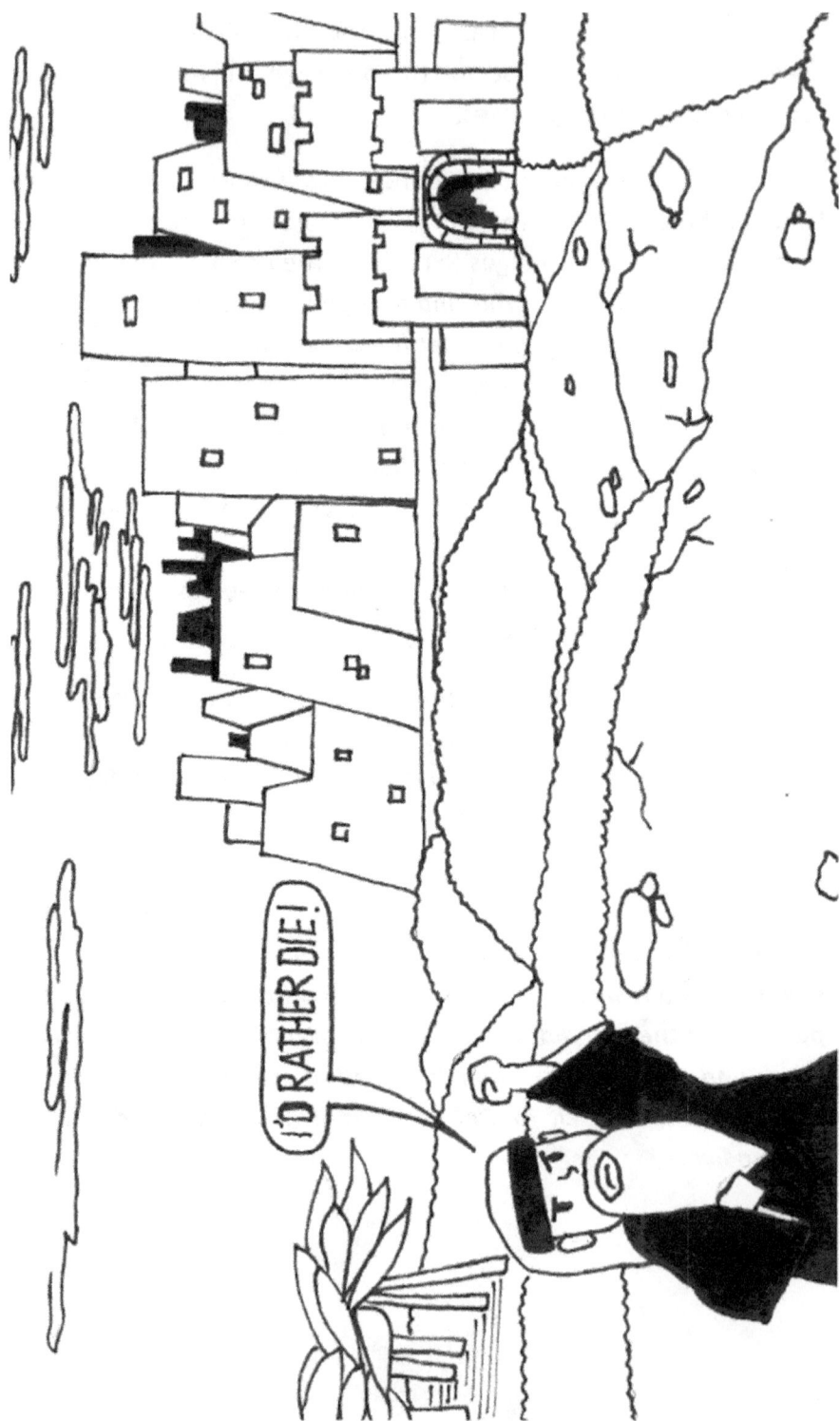

Little did Jonah know that the gourd was meant as an object lesson. The first lesson was on gratitude. Instead of finding joy in God, Jonah misplaced his happiness in his creature comfort. Compare Jonah to what David wrote in Psalm 43:4, *"Then will I go unto the altar of God, unto God my exceeding joy: yea, upon the harp will I praise thee, O God my God."* So, God took away the blessing of the gourd and destroyed the plant with a voracious grub in just one verse. This reminds us to be mindful to give thanks to God for every blessing. We should not place our trust in worldly comforts, such as our stalls and gourds, as these can easily be destroyed by something as small and insignificant as a grub that we may not see coming.

God also brought the heat and an east wind to fan the heat. An east wind is a symbol of judgment, as seen in Psalm 48:7. In a humorous turn of events, Jonah became the one being judged, rather than the Ninevites. The heat sapped his energy and he was miserable, wishing to die again. However, Jonah was not repentant. If he couldn't have the gourd, he would rather die with it. This type of bargaining with God never ends well for anyone.

Jonah 4:9 And God said to Jonah, Doest thou well to be angry for the gourd? And he said, I do well to be angry, even unto death.

Seeing his temper tantrum, God asked Jonah if it was good for him to be angry at Him for destroying the gourd covering. This question led to the next lesson on compassion. Jonah walked right into God's "classroom."

Jonah couldn't understand why God had killed the gourd that was necessary for his comfort or why God had given it to him in the first place. He was also confused as to why God had subjected him to misery again. Jonah was so angry at God that he wished God would kill him as well and put him out of his misery. Have you ever been in this situation or know someone who has? Remember Job in the Bible? What did he say when God took everything away from him? *Job 1:21 And said, Naked came I out of my mother's womb, and naked shall I return thither: the LORD gave, and the LORD hath taken away; blessed be the name of the LORD.* In the end, it worked out very well for Job. *Job 42:12 So the LORD blessed the latter end of Job more than his beginning: for he had fourteen thousand sheep, and six thousand camels, and a thousand yoke of oxen, and a thousand she asses. ¹³ He had also seven sons and three daughters.*

Jonah 4:10 Then said the LORD, Thou hast had pity on the gourd, for the which thou hast not laboured, neither madest it grow; which came up in a night, and perished in a night: ¹¹ And should not I spare Nineveh, that great city, wherein are more than sixscore thousand persons that cannot discern between their right hand and their left hand; and also much cattle?

God dispensed His lesson on compassion to Jonah. Since Jonah had compassion on a short-lived plant that he didn't put any effort into planting and growing, how much more should God pity the souls of men and women, including the souls of over 120,000 innocent children in the great city of Nineveh? And what about the lives of the animals that would be affected by the judgment?

Jonah was left without an answer. Hopefully, he took the lesson to heart.

The Bible is silent about what happened to Jonah after this event. Today, the Nabi Younus shrine in Mosul claims to be Jonah's final resting place. (Muslims claim Jonah as one of their prophets, referred to as Nabi Younus in the Quran.) If this is true, it is unclear how a Jew who hated the Assyrians ended up staying and being buried in Nineveh.

Well, I hope you have enjoyed this book and learned something from it. Most importantly, I hope you can see Jesus in the book of Jonah.

My prayer is that you will grow in grace and in the knowledge of our Lord and Savior Jesus Christ.

To God be the glory, now and forever. Amen.

Appendix A – How to Accept Jesus Christ as Lord & Savior

There is a worldwide epidemic of unhappiness that often leads to depression and even suicidal thoughts. God created each and every one of us to have a relationship with Him, as He desires our love and devotion. However, we often prioritize ourselves and conform to worldly thinking, which never leads to true happiness.

Proverbs 3:13 says, *"Happy is the man that findeth wisdom, and the man that getteth understanding."* This wisdom and understanding can only come from a personal relationship with Jesus Christ as our Lord and Savior. To establish this relationship, we must start at the beginning: we must be born again. *John 3:3 Jesus answered and said unto him, Verily, verily, I say unto thee, Except a man be born again, he cannot see the kingdom of God.*

The path to rebirth is simple. Here are the things you must understand:

- Problem of mankind
  Sin has ruined everything. Our first birth was defective. *Romans 3:23 For all have sinned, and come short of the glory of God.* Read Romans 5:12 and Psalm 51:5. Given that we were all born with a sin nature, our natural selves are not patchable or repairable by worldly or physical means. No amount of education, religion, morality, or good works can erase sin and secure a right relationship with God. Read Ephesians 2:8-9, Romans 11:6, and Hebrews 11:6.

- Penalty of sin

  The Bible says, *"The wages of sin is death."* Sinners who die in their sins are eternally separated from God. Their unrighteous souls will stand in judgment and be found guilty 100% of the time, and they will burn in the lake of fire for eternity. **Ezekiel 18:4** *Behold, all souls are mine; as the soul of the father, so also the soul of the son is mine:* <u>*the soul that sinneth, it shall die*</u>. All unregenerated sinners will die a second death. As the faithful saying goes, "If you are born once, you will die twice; if you are born twice, you will die once." Read Hebrews 9:27, Isaiah 64:6, John 8:23-24, and Revelation 20:11-15.

- Provision of God

  John 3:16 says, *"For God so loved the world, that he gave his only begotten Son, that whosoever believeth in him should not perish, but have everlasting life."* Salvation is God's free gift made available only through Jesus Christ. **Romans 6:23** *For the wages of sin is death; but the gift of God is eternal life through Jesus Christ our Lord.*

Our greatest necessity is to be born again by the Holy Spirit of God, through faith in Jesus Christ. Spiritual birth is a distinct operation of the Spirit, unlike the first birth by flesh. Jesus said, *"That which is born of the flesh is flesh; and that which is born of the Spirit is spirit"* (John 3:6). Although spiritual birth is invisible, the evidence should be clear.

Being saved or born again is based on the knowledge of Christ's life, death, and resurrection combined with faith, and not on feelings, good works, visions, experiences, or membership in a particular religion or denomination. Unfortunately, many people base their beliefs on their feelings and experiences, rather than on biblical truth.

You need to understand that you are a sinner, bound for hell, and that God loves you. He sent His Son to die for your sins, and salvation is a free gift available only in Jesus Christ. *John 14:6 Jesus saith unto him, I am the way, the truth, and the life: no man cometh unto the Father, but by me.*

Salvation is a transaction that requires a conscious decision to exchange sin and death for forgiveness and eternal life. However, it is essential to be careful, as many people claim to be Christians who are not truly saved. Their salvation testimonies are uncertain or incorrect. False claims of saving faith include surviving a terrible accident or near-death experience, speaking in tongues, water baptism, good works, church membership, familiarity with Jesus' stories, someone praying for them, and so on. One time, when I asked a man if he knew the Lord, he replied, "Oh, I was baptized when I was 12." He was basing his salvation on his baptism and living with a false hope. Just when I thought I had heard everything, a young lady claimed to be a Christian because she prayed and God healed her sick dog.

To test the authenticity of one's faith, ask this question: If God were to ask you why He should let you into heaven, what would you say?

To be born again, one must accept Jesus Christ as their Lord and Savior by faith through a simple prayer with the following understanding:

- Admission of sin before Jesus Christ. Jesus is of no use to the self-righteous, just as doctors are of no use to sick people who refuse to admit they are sick (Mark 2:17). You must see yourself as lost before you can be saved.

- Understanding that the penalty of sin is death.

84

- Realizing that only Jesus Christ can forgive sins (1Timothy 2:5, John 14:6, 1John 2:23, 1John 5:11-13, Acts 4:10-12, Matthew 7:13-14).

- Agreeing that God's salvation is a free gift and not a loan or debt that should be repaid through good works. All that is necessary is to simply receive the gift with a sincere prayer and a believing heart. A gift is free to the recipient. The giver is the one who pays the price. God's salvation is a free gift that is dearly paid for by Christ's blood shed on the cross.

- Accepting Jesus Christ as Lord and Savior by faith through a simple prayer. **Romans 10:9** *That if thou shalt confess with thy mouth the Lord Jesus, and shalt believe in thine heart that God hath raised him from the dead, thou shalt be saved. (10) For with the heart man believeth unto righteousness; and with the mouth confession is made unto salvation.*

After accepting Christ as Lord and Savior for the forgiveness of sins, one becomes a child of God. The next step is to be baptized, learn the Bible, and be discipled. It is important to pray for God to send a spiritually mature person to disciple you. If you prayed the above prayer for the first time after reading this book, I welcome you to God's family. Please drop me a note at FishyGospel@yahoo.com to inform me of your decision.

Works Cited

- Matthew Henry's Complete Commentary on the Bible

- John Gill's Exposition on the Whole Bible

- Jamieson, Fausset, and Brown's Commentary on the Whole Bible

About the Author

I grew up in a small fishing village in northern Malaysia, near the border with Thailand. My family practiced Taoism in a predominantly Muslim country. We worshiped idols and honored our ancestors. My father maintained three altars at home for the gods of wealth, the earth, and our ancestors. He offered daily offerings of tea, oil for the lamps, and incense in the morning and evening, seeking protection and blessings from the gods and ancestors. On festival days, he set out meat offerings of chicken or duck and sweet cakes, which would later become our dinner.

We visited temples on special occasions, such as for fortune-telling, to celebrate the birthdays of our favorite gods, to determine the best dates for travel, weddings, building, moving, or starting a new business, and to request healing and financial blessings, usually in the form of lucky lottery numbers. In fact, everyone I knew asked for the same three things: wealth, health, and more wealth. No one ever knelt before an idol to confess, "Forgive me, I am a sinner."

I was frequently ill during my early years, and my grandmother would often take me to the temple, located only about 100 yards away. At one point, the priest decided that I should be adopted by the god of heaven, and I became the god's charge. This meant I had to appear before the god of heaven once a year with offerings and thanksgiving. I can't recall if my health improved, but I survived nonetheless. When I was 15, my grandmother decided that I needed to be redeemed from the god of heaven in order to thrive. Although it meant little to me, I did as I was told. I went to the temple with incense and offerings, expressing my gratitude to the god of heaven for his protection, and informing him that I no longer needed his help.

Our understanding of gods and ghosts was straightforward. We believed in them and did not want to offend them. They could be for us or against us, so we worshiped and made offerings to them for our own benefit.

Hell is real, according to those who practice Taoism in Asia. My grandparents taught me this belief in my childhood. When Christians in the U.S. told me I would go to hell, it wasn't new information.

In Taoism, it is believed that the hell god will judge the dead based on their actions. Those with great good deeds will cross the golden bridge without punishment and be reincarnated as privileged humans. Those with more good deeds than bad will cross the silver bridge without punishment but be reincarnated with fewer privileges. Those who have lived a bad life will be punished and tormented in hell.

I was taught that punishments for deceased relatives in hell could be reduced by burning offerings of hell money, paper houses, cars, and maids made of bamboo and paper. I witnessed my dad perform this ritual shortly after my grandpa passed away. He burned large stacks of high-denomination hell notes, some worth as much as $2 billion each. The total amount must have been in the billions. I was struck by how costly things must be in the afterlife. After the ritual, a small whirlwind appeared and collected the ashes. Although I was frightened, my dad reassured me that the offerings had been received by the hell god.

The Wheel of Reincarnation and the Pavilion of Forgetfulness are located in the Tenth Court of Hell. Sinners who have served their sentence arrive at the Tenth Court to receive their final judgment from the hell god. Afterwards, they are taken to the Pavilion of Forgetfulness where Meng Po, an old lady, serves them a cup of magic tea that makes them forget their past lives. They then go through the Wheel of Reincarnation where some are reborn as humans and some as animals, depending on their past deeds. Some are reincarnated into comfortable lives, while others into lives of suffering.

Life in a small fishing village was good, slow, and peaceful. People were familiar with each other and often visited each other without prior arrangement. My family didn't have much. I spent a lot of time at my neighbor's house watching black and white TV. It was a piece of furniture with a small tube. I remember watching shows like Wild, Wild West, Gun Smoke, Bonanza, The Andy Griffith Show, Looney Tunes, and Disney programs. To this day, I have a fondness for Bugs Bunny.

Behind closed doors in many Chinese families, parents apply intense pressure on their children to succeed. My own parents often compared me to my peers, and when I didn't perform well in school, they would call me "lousy," "stupid," and "useless." While harsh, this was their way of pushing me, preparing me for the challenges of the real world, and aligning with the attitudes of many Chinese parents of their generation.

Despite the difficulties, I now recognize that this pressure helped me face competition on a global level. The pressure came from two main sources: 1) the official retirement age of 55, particularly for males, who must achieve success by age 30, leaving little time for leisure; and 2) a materialistic society in which people are judged by their possessions. A Chinese male who doesn't own a house, a Mercedes-Benz, and a Rolex watch by age 30 is considered a failure. Given that these items cost several times more in Asia than in the U.S., it's tough for those who haven't accumulated wealth by 30 to find a partner. This emphasis on material success led me to believe that life was about making fast and abundant money, by any means necessary, and I eventually joined the materialistic society.

I was transferred to Kuala Lumpur, the capital of Malaysia, for higher education during my freshman year. The transition was challenging, as I went from the serene and beautiful South China Sea beaches to a fast-paced urban environment. I had to quickly adapt to new customs and ways of life, as my background made me stand out among the city dwellers. I struggled with unfamiliar activities like disco dancing and break dancing while holding a stereo the size of small luggage. However, I eventually adjusted and excelled in school. Unfortunately, I was also exposed to the five vices of happiness—eating, drinking, womanizing, gambling, and smoking, which were widely accepted as markers of a successful and happy man.

During my college years, my parents sent my siblings to Kuala Lumpur for education and bought a house for us to live in. My sister became the first Christian in my family after attending St. Mary's girls' school. My parents later retired and moved in with us. The next thing I knew, mom was reading the Bible. This created a rift in my family, as the women embraced Christianity and the men remained Taoist. This led to me harboring resentment towards the Christian religion and my Christian friends, and I treated them poorly.

I was one of the first computer science graduates in Malaysia and had secured a job in the field before I graduated. Back then, personal computers were still a new concept and it required two people to carry an 80 MB hard drive. I regret not keeping my Apple II and Mac. To reminisce about the good old days, I still have a collection of punch cards and hard drives the size of a large pizza.

However, I became increasingly dissatisfied with the government's open discrimination against Chinese and Indian communities, so I decided to move abroad. I had the option of choosing between Australia and the U.S., and since I had grown up watching American TV programs, I chose to come to the US in 1990 with the hope of experiencing cowboys and making enough money to return to Malaysia to live like a king.

Life in the U.S. was a reboot and challenging in the beginning. I found myself having to adjust to a new culture once again. I ended up in Kansas City and was charmed by the place and its people. The residents of the Midwest were incredibly friendly and helpful.

One day, a coworker invited me to church, and I agreed because she was my supervisor. Although I can't recall what was said during the service, I stepped forward during the invitation and was greeted by Pastor Gary Staab. He offered to teach me the Bible, and we met every Saturday morning for about a year. During these lessons, I learned about the basic doctrines and principles of the Bible, and realized for the first time the significance of my sins. (I had previously thought that sin was not a big deal, as I believed that the gods could be bribed and that there was reincarnation.) I learned that my sins separated me from God and that all of my good deeds were unable to cleanse me or provide the required redemption. I searched for answers in my old religion, but none of the idols, monks, or priests could provide me with eternal life. I discovered that eternal life was a gift from God through Jesus Christ. In 1994, I accepted Jesus Christ as my Lord and Savior by faith for the pardoning of my sins.

God is sovereign. A Taoist kid from a small, unknown fishing village set out in search of worldly success and happiness, but by God's grace, found eternal life, true wealth, peace, and purpose. I am forever grateful to the Lord Jesus Christ. I am also thankful for the faithful people whom God placed in my life to teach and guide me in His truth.

I am currently serving the Lord in Hawaii, with a focus on teaching people how to study the Bible. I am also active in India, partnering with local pastors to fulfill the Great Commission. If you have any comments or suggestions, please feel free to reach out to me at FishyGospel@yahoo.com.

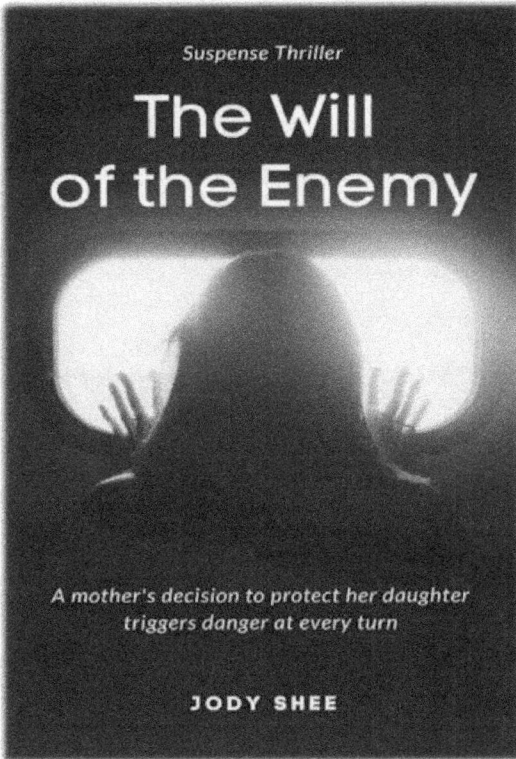

An Inspirational
Suspense Novel

by Jody Shee
available on
Amazon

In 1987, Julie Bradley kidnaps her daughter, stunning everyone who knows her. She has no other alternative to keep her abusive ex-husband from getting at their daughter. Julie's policeman ex-father-in-law wants his granddaughter back, in spite of the horrific things his son has done to her. Like bloodhounds, law enforcement is always one heart-pounding step behind them. For how long can they escape? Will Julie's primitive motherly instincts be enough to match the will of the enemy? Three things keep Julie grounded: her journal, a Psalm, and her daughter. One thing is certain, they will never live ordinary lives.

Jody Shee

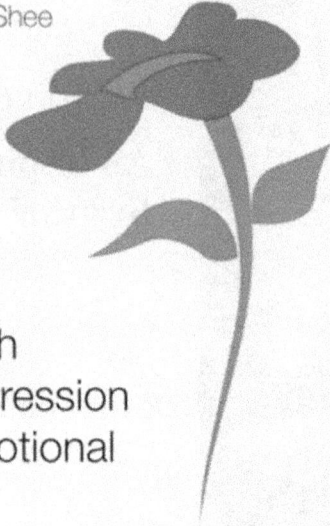

**Ditch
Depression
Devotional**

*31 Days to Biblical Hope, Peace
and Emotional Balance*

A Month-long
Devotional
Guide to Biblical
Hope, Peace and
Emotional
Balance

by Jody Shee
available on
Amazon

Depression does not take God by surprise. What seems like a crisis to us is an opportunity to Him. Relief starts with an understanding of His viewpoint. This 31-day devotional looks at the topic of depression four ways: Common causes; depression's spiritual benefits (there are some!); God's loving rescue; and Bible character overcomers. This book is especially useful to new believers, singles and moms. Besides a short daily reading, it includes: Daily "going deeper" sections for those who want to explore the topic further; a life-altering assignment to complete by the end of the book; links to helpful songs; and online free frameable verse pictures. While it is meant for personal use to complete in one month, it is also appropriate for use in a classroom or small-group setting with a free online leader's guide available on mastertruth.com.

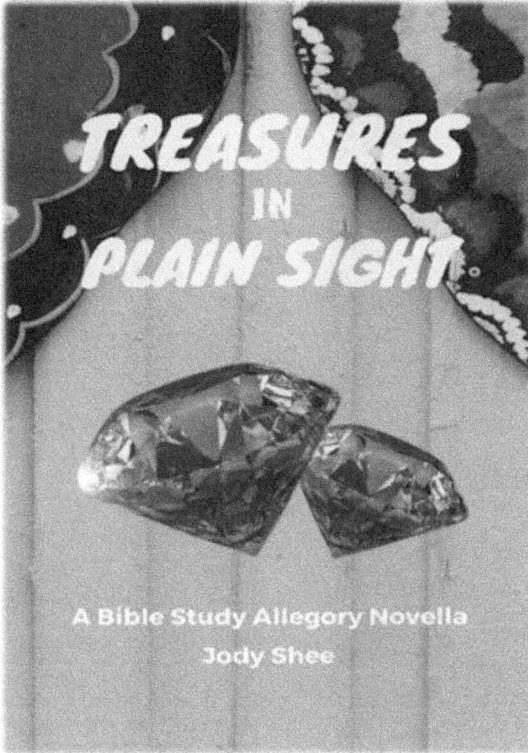

A 56-page Bible Study Allegory Novel

by Jody Shee available on Amazon

If you feel like you're shriveling up spiritually even though you go to church and read your Bible, it's possible you are missing some spiritual keys. Don't worry. I'm not talking about an "experience" you must have. I'm talking about having the eyes of your understanding opened.

In this small book, go on a spiritual journey with Curious Blue to the very heart of God's truth to see Him in a whole new dimension through the illuminating power of His word.

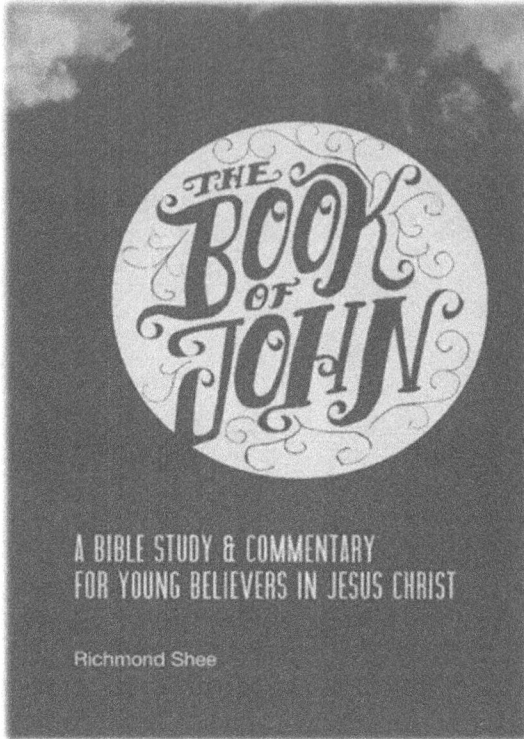

A Commentary
on the Gospel of
John

by Richmond
Shee available
on Amazon

"Read the Gospel of John," is the advice often given to young believers in Jesus Christ. Richmond Shee, a former Buddhist, received the same advice many years ago. In this book, he sets out to show the rich, three-dimensional nature of the Gospel of John, covering the historical, inspirational, and prophetic angles in each chapter, which are frequently revealed in pictures, types, and numbers. He includes illustrations throughout to summarize truth in a simple, inviting way—something visual learners do not have with other commentaries. The book is also filled with verse cross-references, allowing the reader to dig deeper on any topic at any time. The layout of each chapter serves as an example to the reader of how to systematically outline and study a book of the Bible. Get ready for a lively look at the Gospel of John.

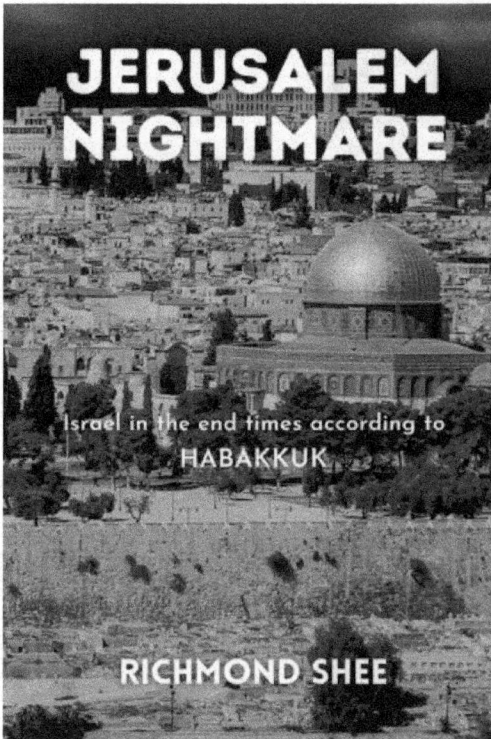

JERUSALEM NIGHTMARE

Israel in the end times according to
HABAKKUK

RICHMOND SHEE

Israel in the End
Times according
to Habakkuk

by Richmond Shee
available on
Amazon

As you delve into the ominous pages of "Jerusalem Nightmare," be prepared to confront the terrifying truth that lies within. Its penetrating analysis of the ancient book of Habakkuk foretells a grim fate for Israel in the end times, where written prophecies portend both doom and salvation. The antichrist and the false prophet will rise, luring Israel into a web of deceit and corruption. The satanic trinity will be unleashed upon Israel, whipping up a storm of death and destruction upon the Jews. As the pages turn, a chilling revelation emerges: Jerusalem, the Holy City, is the "MYSTERY, BABYLON THE GREAT, THE MOTHER OF HARLOTS AND ABOMINATIONS OF THE EARTH." But all hope is not lost. The book also reveals four awe-inspiring visions of the second coming of Jesus Christ, who will descend from the heavens to save the nation of Israel from utter annihilation. Brace yourself for an epic battle between good and evil as you turn each page of "Jerusalem Nightmare."

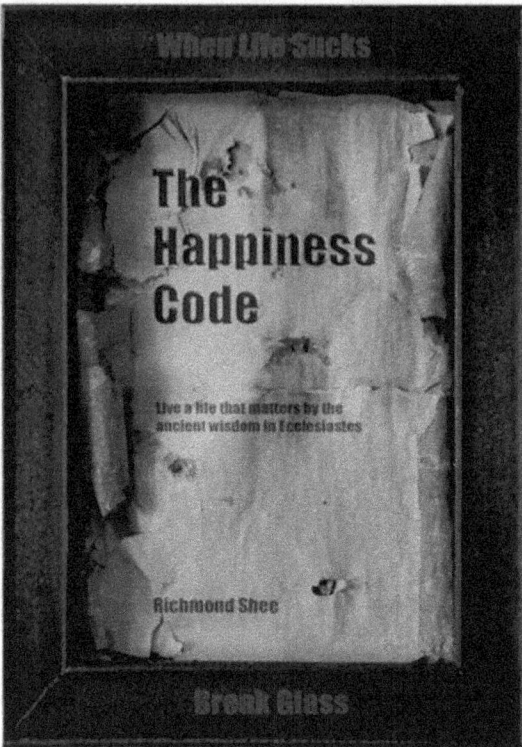

A Commentary
on Ecclesiastes

by Richmond
Shee available
on Amazon

Ever wonder why you remain empty and can't seem to find happiness no matter what you do? Is your anxiety and depression getting worse, and the pain of emptiness just won't go away?

Find out why it is absolutely impossible to be happy by following your own devices. God challenges you to take your best shot at manufacturing happiness and see how life works out for you.

Discover God's way for happiness according to the Bible book of Ecclesiastes, which was authored by King Solomon, the wisest and richest man who ever lived. "The Happiness Code" shows how real happiness is easily attainable. It leads you on a journey through Ecclesiastes where you will find the mind of God, as well as learned lessons from Solomon.

Experience REAL HAPPINESS now!

www.ingramcontent.com/pod-product-compliance
Lightning Source LLC
Chambersburg PA
CBHW020555030426
42337CB00013B/1102